THE SAN FELICE

THE SAN FELICE

A PLAY IN FIVE ACTS

by

MAURICE DRACK

From the Novel by Alexandre Dumas, Père

Translated and Adapted by

FRANK J. MORLOCK

THE BORGO PRESS

An Imprint of Wildside Press LLC

MMIX

www.wildsidepress.com

FIRST WILDSIDE EDITION

CONTENTS

DEDICATION

To

MY BELOVED GABY

With Special Thanks

to

PATRICIA TETER and IBETTE SANTANA

CAST OF CHARACTERS

King Ferdinand IV of the Two Sicilies
Salvato Palmieri
Cardinal Ruffo
Michele the Mad
Brother Pacifico
Admiral Caracciolo
Nicolino Caracciolo
Chevalier San Felice
Doctor Cyrillo
Championnet
Hector Caraffa
Lord Nelson
Garat
Crown Attorney Vanni
Pasquale de Simone
Beccaio
The Bambino
D'Ascoli
Acton
Ariola
Mammone

The Doyen of the Chapter of Saint Janvier
Andre Baker
Regulus
Luisa San Felice
Marie Caroline
Lady Hamilton
Nanno
Fragola
Angiolina
Dona Euphemia
La Quaglia
Cecilia
Lords and Ladies of the Court
Soldiers, *Lazzaroni* (Loafers), Sailors, French and Neapolitan citizens, etc.

ACT I

SCENE 1

The Action takes place in Naples from September 1798 to July 1799.

The Quay and port of Mergellina at Naples. To the left, the villa of San Felice with a gallery forming a balcony on the first floor. The palms of the garden dominate the house. Further back, a public fountain surrounded by a stone bench. To the right, merchant shops which sprawl around the square. To the extreme right the outline of the Palace of Queen Joanna rises from a rock which dominates the sea. At the extreme back a panoramic view of Naples and the port.

At rise characters promenade through the market. Fragola walks across the square with her basket full of flowers. The Bambino, squatting down, plays with young lazzaroni (loafers) of his own age.

WATER SELLER: Fresh water—iced. Who wants water? (*circulating*)

WOMAN IN THE MARKET: Buy one of these beautiful watermelons from me, signor. You won't find better at the new market.

SECOND MARKET WOMAN: Violet pears, the true pear of Pouzzoli.

BAMBINO: I won!

THE LOSER: (*to those who surround him*) Cursed Bambino, he played a trick on me.

BAMBINO: (*laughing*) That's the fate of the clumsy. Do you want your revenge? Double or nothing. If I win again, I will regale Fragola, my ward.

LOSER: With the Madonna's grace, I begin. (*they start playing again. The group around them tightens up*)

HECTOR CARAFFA: The message says: "Three o'clock at the Mergellina." Championnet's envoy has this identifying word. Rome. And I will reply: Naples.

NICOLINO CARACCIOLO: How will he know us?

HECTOR: By this.

NICOLINO: A red rose, a jonquil, and a sunflower.

HECTOR: The three colors of the future flag of Naples. But if Championnet has chosen the man that I suspect he won't need this sign to come straight to us.

NICOLINO: A friend?

HECTOR: A brother in arms, a fellow countryman.

NICOLINO: His aide-de-camp, Salvato Palmieri. I know him. Exiled, condemned to death by the Bourbon, France has become his second country. But he hasn't forgotten that he's the child of Naples, and he's put his sword in the service of the great republic, because he hopes the French will deliver Naples from their tyrant. Brave Salvato.

HECTOR: Silence! That's the name of one proscribed; it's not prudent to pronounce it in the open street. (*they move away*)

PASQUALE: (*to Beccaio*) Our man came through the Capua gate an hour ago.

BECCAIO: Are you sure of it?

PASQUALE: By God! An aide-de-camp of General Championnet in full uniform doesn't go through the streets of Naples every day. He went to the Embassy first.

BECCAIO: And that's a place of asylum. There he will be in safety.

PASQUALE: Indeed, yes, if he'd found Citizen Garat there and been able to deliver his dispatches. But the Ambassador has absented himself since dawn so as not to be present at the reception being prepared for Lord Nelson.

BECCAIO: Ah! Ah!

PASQUALE: Our officer, to kill time, at this moment is sauntering through the town. And we will find a way to involve him in some brawl.

BECCAIO: (*pulling his knife*) Where we will trim his buttons.

PASQUALE: Oh! The important thing is to seize his dispatches. (*they slip into the crowd.*)

FRAGOLA: Ah, Signor Nicolino Caracciolo, the Admiral's nephew, my best client.... (*runs to Nicolino.*) Signor, would you like this beautiful bouquet of Jasmin from Sorrento? Surrounded by violets from Parma?

NICOLINO: No, pretty one. Simply attach to my coat this red Camelia, this rose jonquil, and these three forget-me-nots—with your little hand.

FRAGOLA: All done.

NICOLINO: And take this new scudo for your trouble.

FRAGOLA: Thanks, signor.

SAN FELICE: (*coming out of his house with Doctor Cyrillo*) There's no need to be uneasy?

CYRILLO: The Signora San Felice is of a delicate sensibility—she must have had some intense emotion—

SAN FELICE: Frightful, my dear Cyrillo. The horrible assassination of Don Clemente was recounted to her without any warning. Strangled under the pretext he was a Jacobin.

CYRILLO: That is to say suspected by the Neapolitan Court.

SAN FELICE: She wasn't even spared the hideous ending of the tragic scene. Mammone, that cannibal, drinking the blood of his victim.

CYRILLO: And that scoundrel walks about freely. The Queen's bailiffs protect him. Happily, the Signora has energy and elasticity, for she's not at the end of her emotions.

SAN FELICE: What do you mean?

CYRILLO: Doesn't the impunity of the assassins tell you whose hand struck the blow?

SAN FELICE: The Queen. (*going towards the back, they vanish.*)

PASQUALE: (*writing*) The Chevalier San Felice, Librarian to the King, in intimate conversation with Doctor Cyrillo, known Jacobin. Note that.

BAMBINO: Won again! Long Live! Ten baioques coming to me. (*gathering his winnings and running to the merchants.*) Watermelons, figs, oranges. (*returning with his hands full.*) Hey, Fragola, come quick.

FRAGOLA: (*running*) Holy Mother! That's for me, Carlino mio, how sweet you are.

BAMBINO: (*sitting on a bench*) Sit down good daughter, and sharpen your pretty teeth. (*squatting at her feet*)

MICHELE: (*appearing in the midst of one group*) The entire fleet destroyed, I tell you. There's not one French vessel in the Bay of Aboukir. Their damned General Bonaparte is a prisoner thanks to Lord Nelson.

THE LAZZARONI: Long live Lord Nelson!

MICHELE: Also, as today is the day the great man, the hero of Aboukir is disembarking in Naples, we will carry him in triumph to the palace.

LAZZARONI: Bravo!

MICHELE: Long live Lord Nelson!

LAZZARONI: Long live Lord Nelson!

NICOLINO: (*returning with Hector*) That's right, good beasts, acclaim your Nelson. He'll make sure you pay the expenses of his glory. You hear them?

HECTOR: You'd have to be decidedly deaf!

NICOLINO: And it's with the likes of these you intend to make a free people?

HECTOR: Bah! You make statues out of clay.

NICOLINO: The day our heads are chopped off, they'll be eagerly yelling Bravo.

HECTOR: What's it matter? If we've succeeded in burning down this edifice of oppression and iniquity? The blood of martyrs makes good semen.

NICOLINO: Eh! eh! When you talk of the scaffold, here comes the purveyor of it, Master Pasquale de Simone, Bailiff of the Queen, who seems to be brooding on us with his eye—both of them.

HECTOR: My dear fellow, to plot in the open street is still the best way I've found of confusing spies. (*going back*)

MICHELE: (*rapping on a window of the Villa San Felice*) Angiolina.

ANGIOLINA: (*leaning out the window*) It's you, Michele. Come upstairs quick. The Signora is asking for you.

MICHELE: (*hoisting himself up to the window*) I have only a second. Tell my little sister that Nanno will come here at nightfall.

ANGIOLINA: (*astonished*) Nanno, the Albanian! Jesus! Mary! Nanno, the witch!

MICHELE: Eh! Even if she were the creature of the devil, Luisa wants her, and whatever Luisa wants must be done.

ANGIOLINA: Michele, take care—you love her, too much.

MICHELE: Jealous! Luisa is my milk sister. If I am good for anything it's to her that I owe it. Thanks to her my poor mother never lacked anything. Also, my life belongs to her. She can take it. But my heart belongs to you, ingrate!—and you know that quite well.

ANGIOLINA: She has the best part. You'll end by making me hate her.

MICHELE: (*embracing her and leaping to the ground*) Until tonight, stubborn girl. They're waiting for me at the port.

BAMBINO: (*to a poultry seller*) Now here's a lady goose, Mama La Quaglia, who will produce a majestic effect on the skewer.

LA QUAGLIA: Well! Bambino, for a pair of scudi you can have the joy of roasting it.

BAMBINO: La Quaglia, my hands are not filled with scudi. But I have a mouth full of good advice. And if you don't want your goose to fly off , may that fine hare from Persano beat it without saying boo, accompanied by a brace of partridges, a number of quail, and some few dozen thrushes—It's time to close your shop.

LA QUAGLIA: What's that mean? Dumb joke?

BAMBINO: Eh! Eh! Saint Francis is a great Saint and the brother collector of the Convent of Saint Ephrem knows some beautiful things.

LA QUAGLIA: (*with terror*) Brother Pacifico.

BAMBINO: (*pointing to an alley*) Look, he arrives in the market with his donkey, his talisman in his hand. You know, that lucky belt of Saint Francis. He has only to rest it on your goose, and it's not in the King's kitchen that it will see the fire. A word to the wise is enough.

LA QUAGLIA: (*rushing to hide her best pieces*) Mercy. Saint Janvier protect us!

BAMBINO: (*laughing*) He won't protect you against Saint Francis. The saints don't eat each other, my old gossip.

(*A crowd of women, children, and lazzaroni rush in ahead of Fra Pacifico who beats out a passage in the midst of them, arriving on his donkey.*)

ALL: Fra Pacifico

NICOLINO: (*to Hector*) The Brother Collector of the Capuchins. By God, we're going to laugh. Observe the terrified faces of all the market folk.

HECTOR: Watch your tongue especially. You can feel the storm here.

YOUNG WOMAN: Your blessing, Father.

PACIFICO: (*caressing the girl's chin*) Two for one, at your service my pretty penitent. (*giving her his hand to kiss after having blessed her*)

OLD WOMAN: Your hand to kiss, holy man.

PACIFICO: Here's the belt, old woman. (*giving her the belt to kiss.*) Come on, come on.

FIRST LAZZARONI: In the name of Saint Francis, a winning number for the lottery.

PACIFICO: Try number seven, it's the holy number.

SECOND LAZZARONI: A double five.

THIRD LAZZARONI: Nothing but luck for me.

PACIFICO: (*flourishing an enormous laurel stick that he holds in his hand and striking the ground forcefully*) Peace! You are deafening me and make room for Jacobino. (*some of the children and young lazzaroni hold the donkey and feed him leaves of carrots and cabbages.*)

LAZZARONI: Jacobino.

SECOND LAZZARONI: Funny name for a donkey!

PACIFICO: He's just a Jacobin, my son, because he's a restive donkey, always in revolt, a glutton, wanton, lecherous, and impious!

THE LAZZARONI: (*laughing*) Bravo, Don Pacifico!

PACIFICO: (*brandishing his baton*) The beast knows what his name costs him in awful corporal punishments. Jacobino pays for his colleagues the Jacobins of Naples, while waiting the opportunity in their turn for me to put them under my bludgeon—their flesh and backs.

BAMBINO: Yes, they must be chastised with blows from a stick.

PACIFICO: And this is not my first attempt. At Toulon, where I was a sailor aboard the Minerva, I roughed up more than one of those sans culottes.

NICOLINO: Why does that clown seem to be looking at us when he says that?

THE LAZZARONI: We need to rough up those of Naples, as well.

PACIFICO: And that cannot be too soon, you see. Too many are found in the streets with these trousers, without boots, with unpowdered hair, and French style suits. When the dance begins, I will undertake to play the First part in the orchestra.

NICOLINO: (*advancing, very politely*) And who then will you make dance in such a pretty way, my reverend father of God?

PACIFICO: (*scrutinizing him*) Who, signor? Why all the fops who do their hair like Titus, deny God and Saint Janvier, and conspire on a daily basis against the Queen. In a word, all the Jacobins of Naples.

NICOLINO: Ah, fie, my father. What has become of your Christian charity? You mistreat these poor Jacobins.

PACIFICO: By the blood of Saint Janvier, they deserve to be!

NICOLINO: Do you think so? Well, as for me, knowing them, I look on them differently, reverend father.

PACIFICO: By the Holy Cross, we would be curious to hear you defend them, signor. Right everybody?

THE LAZZARONI: (*grumbling*) He's one of them; he's a Jacobin.

PACIFICO: Silence and listen. I am here to reply.

NICOLINO: Well, very dear Capuchin father, a Jacobin is a man who loves his country. (*murmurs*) Who wishes for the good of the people. (*exclamations*) Who asks for the same laws for the great and the small, liberty for everyone, and the same duties for everybody. (*murmurs*) A Jacobin asks that no one be oppressed and pressured, and finds it odious when poor merchants, poor fishermen, and brave farmers—like these who are listening to us from their shops—who have worked hard to bring their produce to market, have an idle monk steal boldly from them in the name of Saint Francis, the best part of their profits and the most beautiful displays from their windows.

PACIFICO: (*furious*) He's an atheist!

LAZZARONI: Yes, yes, an atheist.

HECTOR: Now we're in good shape, thanks to your cursed tongue.

PACIFICO: He's a heretic; he insulted Saint Francis!

(*Nicolino shrugs his shoulders and turns his back on the lazzaroni who follow him vociferating with him, but who do not dare lay a hand on him. The circle presses, bit by bit, around Nicolino and Hector. At this moment Salvato enters from the back and comes forward to determine what is happening. Luisa San Felice appears with Angiolina on the balcony. Pascale de Simone and Beccaio follow Salvato.*)

PASQUALE: That crazy Nicolino Caracciolo is going to do our business. The fire's lit and we have only to blow on it.

BECCAIO: (*pointing to Salvato*) Then that is indeed the envoy from General Championnet?

THE LAZZARONI: Down with the Jacobins!

LUISA: (*worried, to Angiolina*) What's all that uproar? What's happening now?

ANGIOLINA: I don't know, signora. Nothing serious, certainly. Some dispute in the market.

PACIFICO: (*whose voice dominates the tumult*) He is himself a Jacobin.

LAZZARONI: Get the Jacobin! Get the Jacobin!

LUISA: You hear them? They are shouting "Get the Jacobin!"

ANGIOLINA: (*wanting to pull her away*) Come, madam.

LUISA: No, no. I want to know what's wrong with them this time. I want to see.

SALVATO: Why, I'm not mistaken; it's Nicolino and Hector.

NICOLINO: (*reaching the fountain, he stands on the bench surrounding it*) You are forgetting, monk, that the first of the Jacobins was called Jesus of Nazareth!

PACIFICO: He's blaspheming. He's a sacrilegious one. A friend of France.

MAMMONE: (*pushing through the crowd*) A friend of the French—where is he? Let me bleed him.

LAZZARONI: (*making way for him*) Mammone! Mammone!

LUISA: (*uttering a cry*) Mammone! that monster!!!

NICOLINO: (*with cold blooded raillery*) Move out of the way so I can see this manner of carnivorous beast you call Mammone.

SALVATO: The scoundrel who assassinated Don Clemente.

MAMMONE: You want to know me? Look.

NICOLINO: I am looking and what astonishes me is not to see wrapped around your neck the rope that should hang you high and fast from the gibbet of Vieux Marche. What could the Public Prosecutor be thinking?

MAMMONE: (*furious*) You know what happens to those who insult me?

NICOLINO: You are much changed, bandit. Today, you can go thirsty. For sure, it's not my blood that will appease it.

MAMMONE: (*brandishing his knife*) We'll see about that!

NICOLINO: (*with a quick blow of his cane, knocking the knife from Mammone's hand*) It's already seen! (*Mammone utters a howl, staggers, and disappears into the crowd to find his knife.*) As for the rest of you, who don't have enough invectives and outrages for patriots, you are really made only to bear a pack saddle eternally, ferocious donkeys that you are. You are really the sons of Pulcinella and the worthy subjects of Nosey. Go on, make way, make way!

MAMMONE: (*reappearing*) Death to the Jacobins!

PACIFICO: Death to the Atheist!

LUISA: O my God! Unfortunate young man— Will no one come to his aid?

NICOLINO: One Hundred knives against two canes. By Jove, my knaves, you are going to remember this.

HECTOR: (*striking to the right and left*) Watch your heads!

SALVATO: To the Devil with diplomatic immunity.

MAMMONE: Death to the Jacobins! Death to the friends of the French!

SALAVATO: (*clubbing the Lazzaroni from his path and joining Hector and Nicolino*) By Jove, rogues, you are going to learn at your own expense how heavy a French sword weighs in the hands of an officer of the Republic.

(*Hector lets out an exclamation of joy and shakes his hand*)

LUISA: (*with a cry of joy*) Ah! see, Lina—that officer.

(*The Lazzaroni, taken aback have recoiled and enlarged the circle.*)

PACIFICO: What, you back off, codardi! Before a Frenchman!

PASQUALE: (*to Beccaio*) Come on; if we don't get involved in it, all these jokers are going to flee.

MAMMONE: A Frenchman! an officer—What luck! I swore to the Madonna, to carve me out a hole in the skull of the first Frenchman who happened by my knife. The rest of you, be bold.

LAZZARONI: (*returning to the charge*) Long Live Mammone! Knife 'em! Knife 'em!

MICHELE: Holy Mother! Why, they're committing murder here!

LUISA: Michele!

MICHELE: Understood, little sister. (*jumping into the middle of the circle*) Hey, there, clumsies, put up your playthings right away!

LAZZARONI: Michele!

MICHELE: Eh, yes. Admiral Caracciolo is on my heels, he's coming with his sailors, the whole company of the

Minerva, and you know he doesn't like anyone taking the law into their own hands.

PACIFICO: (*hesitating*) My admiral.

MICHELE: Who won't pardon you for having laid hands on his nephew.

PACIFICO: His nephew.

MICHELE: (*to Pacifico*) Nicolino Caracciolo who he loves like a son—

PACIFICO: (*scratching his ear*) The Devil. From the moment it's his nephew.— Get back, all of you, get back. (*reaches his donkey*) It's Jacobino who's the cause of all the trouble. (*mauling his donkey*) Hue! Jacobino, Hue, then!

(*The Lazzaroni have dispersed. Mammone gives ground with regret. Admiral Caracciolo arrives with an escort of sailors.*)

MAMMONE: (*to Pasquale, with rage*) The ploy failed.

PASQUALE: (*finger on his lips, making him a sign to be silent*) Eh, no! the game is only delayed. (*they leave.*)

PACIFICO: (*furious*) And with all this my baskets are empty! (*heading his donkey towards the shops which stretch before him, he goes, cordon in hand, rapping hastily on a bunch of supplies, seizing them, and always shouting in a nasal accent as he thrusts them in his basket.*) In the name of Saint Francis. (*disappearing.*)

SALVATO: God—they howl but they don't bite! (*sheathing his sword*)

HECTOR: My dear Captain, if you hadn't come, as always at the right moment, we would have been torn to pieces well and good.

SALVATO: (*pointing to Michele*) It's this brave lad we ought to thank, who with one word made them give ground.

MICHELE: As for me, I was bound to warn them of the trouble they were going to get. The Admiral, they know him—wouldn't have spared them.

NICOLINO: (*coming forward with the Admiral*) Uncle, by whom were you warned of the danger I was running?

FRAGOLA: (*timidly*) By me.

NICOLINO: Fragola.

ADMIRAL: Yes, I learned from this child, that your habitual imprudence had just provoked the wrath of the Lazzaroni of the Mergellina, and I came running.

NICOLINO: By Saint Janvier. Fragola, can I give you a kiss? (*grabbing her by the waist*)

FRAGOLA: (*letting him do it*) Very willingly, signor.

ADMIRAL: I was able to save you this time, dear child, but take care. My credit wanes. The Queen knows me to be the declared adversary of the English Alliance and unable to bend me, will break me one day. Till later. (*to

Hector) Goodbye, Count Ruvo. (*to Salvato*) Your hand, Captain. (*he leaves with his escort of marines*)

HECTOR: (*to Salvato, pulling him*) Well, the general?

SALVATO: Begs you to wait for him and attempt nothing yet.

HECTOR: Wait—still?

SALVATO: Avoid a premature action. We could not support you in it. We have much left to do at Rome. We lack artillery, munitions. Patience, that's what is in the dispatches I am bearing counsel Citizen Garat, who must be exasperated by the arrival of Admiral Nelson.

HECTOR: Patience, same old song and during this time our enemies are each day oiling the gates of the Castle Saint Elmo to shut in one of us. The scaffold is erected permanently on the Square of Vieux Marche. They decapitated Vitigliano for having spoken ill of the favorite.

SALVATO: (*shivering*) Lady Hamilton.

NICOLINO: Yes, that adventuress has consecrated her respectability by means of the executioner's axe. That courtesan is thirsty of veneration. Naples scorns her, she avenges herself. And already, Marie Caroline, finding that justice limps along too slowly; she's come to assassination. Two days ago, Don Clemente—

HECTOR: Poor friend—

NICOLINO: One of the leaders of the liberal party was besieged and butchered in his home, in the court of Naples, by a band of villains having at their head this Mammone. Without your intervention today would have been our turn; they would have dragged our cadavers through the streets; they would have burned them under the windows of the palace to give, as incense, the execrable perfume of human sacrifice to the Austrian woman.

SALVATO: That's frenzy—

HECTOR: It's the delirium of fear. Fear makes ferocity. At the first grumbling of the Revolution in France, Marie Caroline sensed the Neapolitan earth tremble beneath her feet, and made us pay in executions—for her sleepless nights. Whoever stands aside from the coteries of the court is suspect. Whoever dares publicly to judge her politics is condemned. And if they only sacrificed some men, valiant souls are not lacking. But the fortune of the state is delivered to this gang of foreign pillagers—of which, Lady Hamilton is the gallant and impudent *coryphée*. To fill the gorge of this pack, they pressure the bourgeoisie; they ruin the artisan with arbitrary taxes. For these wretches gold suffices. But as for her, it's the domain of the state she tears to shreds. Tomorrow, should she demand Sicily, she will obtain it with a smile and to give over some days to red coats and our ports and our fortresses, a kiss will suffice for that.

SALVATO: (*somberly*) Yes, she's a fatal creature.

NICOLINO: (*astonished*) You know her?

SALVATO: (*embarrassed*) I was able to glimpse her a few years ago in England.— But the King?

NICOLINO: The King, my dear chap, hunts at Caserta or fishes at Pausilippa, and since he's left free in the evening at the Opera, he eats his macaroni in his box—in the manner of Pulcinella. This much rejoices the pit and infinitely raises the royal dignity. When he's not disturbed, and installed at San Leuccio, he reviews the workers of the factory. Drawn from the prettiest girls in the Kingdom. It makes little difference to him what's done in council. When, by chance, he's present at it, it's not unusual that at the first call of his huntsmen, he gives the slip to his ministers. History will catalogue him under the name Ferdinand IV, but his true name is the one the lazzaroni have given him: Colleague Nosey. You have to see him in the midst of them when he sells his fish—for he comes even here, on fishing days to compete with the fish-sellers of the market. (*murmurs in the distance. A large fishing boat puts in at the royal dock, bordering the Mergellina*) And per Dio, you're going to be able to judge, for right now his caravelle is docking at the quay. Listen to the screams of joy of these buffoons of the mob.

THE LAZZARONI: (*running*) It's Nosey! Hey! Nosey. So it's fish day, then! (*huge lackeys in silk stockings and very rich finery, with high, 3 cornered feathered hats bearing trestles lay out the King's fish table, and spread on it the contents of the large baskets that the sailors hand down from the caravelle.*)

KING: D'Ascoli, you will keep the accounts.

D'ASCOLI: Yes, Sire.

FIRST LAZZARONI: Things going good, Nasone?

KING: Very good, children. (*to D'Ascoli*) I want to know exactly how much I make fishing.

MICHELE: And why is that, colleague?

KING: Sonofabitch! You never know what may happen in the times we're living in. One day I may be forced to establish myself.

MICHELE: You will die in the skin of a practical joker.

FIRST LAZZARONI: But look what fish.

BAMBINO: By God. Did he pick the best places to cast his line.

MICHELE: (*taking the King's nose*) Say, colleague Nosey, I think your nose has grown since the last time I saw it.

KING: (*giving him a cuff*) And has my hand grown, too, ruffian?

BAMBINO: (*pulling the pigtail of the King's wig*) In revenge, Nosey, the tail of your wig.

KING: (*giving him a kick*) Sonofabitch! Now here's a kick in the butt you didn't steal, moscherino. And now children, make room, make room. You are all of the race of hornets, you buzz around without making honey. Let the friendly housewives approach at their ease. They bring me beautiful shillings that jingle nicely. I am furiously in need of money, my boy, for this job of monarch is becoming more difficult every day.

MICHELE: Bravo, Pulcinella!

KING: (*imitating the fish merchants*) To the boat! To the boat! To the boat! Who wants beautiful fish, fresh, live? Look come here, touch 'em, feel 'em, my lady; Here this one's still wriggling. You won't find better stuff anywhere. Look at this silver fish. You'd say it was a gold ingot. I have dancing girls at Saint Charles who are less richly dressed. You may prefer this snapper with a red corsage, a pretty fish my little lady. You will place this for me on a bed of flour with garlic sauce and you will bring me news of it. Look here. Here's a mullet, bonita with scales of steel. Look at this sun fish. You'd say it was a Basque drum. It's enough to nourish an economical family for a week, and it will make your lips drool over it.

ANGIOLINA: How much is the mullet?

KING: That one, my pretty child, only for such pretty eyes—will be three scudi.

ANGIOLINA: Three scudi! That's worth twenty-five sols, not any more.

KING: (*hands on his hips*) Twenty-five sols for a three-pound mullet, twenty-five sols! Why look at such effrontery; it makes your eyes melt into lemonade, it pinches the mouth in a chicken's ass and it says to you—twenty-five sols for a mullet. Why, I'd prefer to throw it to the shore. Slut!

ANGIOLINA: Fine! Keep your mullet. I will find a better one at the Vieux Marche.

KING: (*retaining her*) You are going. She's playing naughty. Look, pretty one, you have to pay a nice price to get the plum pickings. Put in ten more. Make it thirty-five.

ANGIOLINA: No, Thirty.

KING: Come on, because it's you. Take it. But it's a gift. Inscribe thirty sols, D'Ascoli. A three-pound mullet. Eh, say, Miss Sorrentino. Two of these coins have been clipped. That doesn't work with me.

ANGIOLONA: Really! Is he tightfisted! Here are two others.

KING: You must be honest, beautiful!

NICOLINO: (*to Salvato*) Now there! He haggles over the price of a mullet. He weighs coins. Exchanges sweet talk with the servants, cuffs with the lazzaroni. And meanwhile, Marie Caroline terrorizes Naples at her leisure and ruins the state.

HECTOR: Come, our friends are waiting for us. We must inform them without delay of the situation in Rome. (*they move away*)

PACIFICO: (*thrashing his donkey*) Hue, Jacobino! Hue, thrice revolutionary! Hue, diabolical fisherman. Do you think we are going to return to the convent without fish? Without fish, a thousand port holes! And tomorrow is a fast day.

KING: (*to D'Ascoli*) Did you write? Three shillings for the silver fish, twenty-five sols for the bonita. Come on, connoisseurs we still have a magnificent tunny. A forty-five-pound tunny. A morsel for a King.

PACIFICO: (*cocking his ear*) A forty-five-pound tunny? What a lucky chance. Great Saint Francis! You watch over your beloved sons. (*he approaches the King's table*)

KING: What! No one says a word? The thing is fat like your purses, my gossips. So be it. We will chop it up to suit you, although, truthfully, it's a shame. D'Ascoli have 'em cut it in four parts for me.

PACIFICO: (*coming forward*) Don't cut it.

KING: A purchaser. Stop. (*looking at Brother Pacifico*) Why, say, monk, do you know that's worth thirty ducats, a fish like that.

PACIFICO: A tunny. Such a vulgar fish. Thirty Ducats! You ought to blush. Nosey and I see that heaven made me emerge immediately to cure you of the sin of avarice.

KING: You, Don Beacier. And how much will you take it for, man of sandals?

PACIFICO: The gifts we receive through Heaven's clemency must be considered by us as a transient deposit.

KING: Do you have thirty ducats?

PACIFICO: And if the blessed Saint Francis caused such a rich prey to fall into your nets, it's because he had pity on the poverty of his faithful servants of the Convent of Saint Ephrem who do not have fish for tomorrow, Friday.

KING: Do you have thirty ducats? Ta, ta, ta, ta—all this chatter has for its conclusion that you don't have one sol in your pockets. Well, instead of being lean, you will be abstinent, my lovelies, which will be infinitely more agreeable to heaven.

PACIFICO: (*extending his belt over the tuna*) In the name of Saint Francis, let no one budge. This belongs to me.

KING: You are saying?

PACIFICO: The belt of the Blessed Saint Francis has touched the fish. This fish here is mine.

KING: Will you beat it? The farce has gone on too long.

PACIFICO: It's my right.

KING: To steal from me?

THE LAZZARONI: It's his right, yes, yes. It's the custom. You're wrong, Nosey. You must respect Saint Francis.

KING: Will you shut up, good-for-nothings!

PACIFICO: (*taking the fish*) The tuna is mine.

KING: (*grabbing him*) Will you let go of that?

PACIFICO: (*pulling harder*) It's up to you to let go. If you don't want to be excommunicated.

D'ASCOLI: (*to the King*) Take care, sire, you must respect the customs. You're going to get yourself in a fight with the Church by giving such a bad example.

KING: And I laugh at that.

(*Cannon fire heard.*)

ARIOLA: (*arriving unexpectedly*) Sire, the English fleet is in sight. Lord Nelson is going to disembark and the Queen prays you to come as fast as possible to join her in receiving him.

KING: (*who has released the tuna*) More drudgery. The devil is with the Queen and her English.

PACIFICO: (*putting the tuna in one of the baskets on Jacobino*) Long live Saint Francis! I am bearing it off!

KING: (*as he leaves*) As for you, Monk, I will be even with you!

(*The cannon continues to thunder. The Lazzaroni leave behind the procession, shouting, "To the Port! Everyone to the Port!" The shops close, the square empties. The day slowly wanes.*)

LUISA: (*leaving her house and taking a few steps towards the quay*) Here the air is less inflamed. The evening breeze sooths me.

ANGIOLINA: (*extending a rug on a bench near the house*) Sit down on this bench, signora.

LUISA: (*returning slowly to sit*) That young officer who threw himself so bravely into the mêlée; he was a French man?

ANGIOLINA: You must believe it. They were shouting death to the French. But, in short, it was Michele who saved them all.

LUISA: Michele is a brave heart and I feel grateful to him for what he did.

ANGIOLINA: (*who is squatting at her feet*) Is it true, Madame, that Michele is going to bring you Nanno?

LUISA: Ah! She will come—what do you want? It's a caprice. She's very clever, so they say. It's the fantasy of an uneasy heart to want to know.

ANGIOLINA: Ah! From the moment that Madame has no fear—

LUISA: Bah! She will tell me follies.

ANGIOLINA: (*rising*) Here he is, Madame, here he is. With his sorceress.

MICHELE: (*to Luisa*) Madame, you were wanting to meet Nanno the prophetess of Pausilippa. I bring her to you. I hope that you will be satisfied with my zeal.

LUISA: Believe me, my friend, I will make it up to you fairly.

NANNO: (*remaining behind, still cloaked in her shawl*) Since when do milk brothers and sisters talk so formally? Those who have hung from the same breast; aren't they as close relations as those who have been carried in the same breast? Talk freely, children. That pleases God to see his creatures love each other. Despite the distance that separates them.

MICHELE: Huh? Did I tell you she is a real sorceress, little sister, and my word, this makes me tremble.

LUISA: Why, Michele?

MICHELE: Ah, now see. Do you know what she predicted to me, not later than last evening? She predicted that I would go to war and that I would become a Colonel.

ANGIOLINA: Colonel.

MICHELE: And that I would be—

ANGIOLINA: (*intrigued*) What then?

MICHELE: Well—that I would be hanged!

ANGIOLINA: Horrors!

LUISA: Are all her predictions so lugubrious?

NANNO: (*always a few steps behind*) O youth! Curious and imprudent youth! Will you always be pushed by a power stronger than your will to out strip the future which rushes so quickly to meet you?

LUISA: Despite myself, I am shivering. Should I renounce knowing—?

NANNO: There's still time. If you are afraid I will leave.

LUISA: No, no—remain.

(*Nanno casts her cloak to her feet and allows her Albanian costume to be seen. She advances towards Luisa and considers her silently for a few seconds.*)

NANNO: Blonde hair, blue eyes, moist, velvety, voluptuous—

LUISA: (*uneasy*) Nanno!

NANNO: Plump hands, delicate golden skin. Oh, beautiful creature, you are indeed consecrated to Venus.

LUISA: (*rising*) Nanno—Nanno!

NANNO: You were born on a Friday. At the hour of midnight. Right?

LUISA: (*astonished*) Indeed. My mother often told me that my first cries were mixed with the reverberations of the clock striking twelve—which separated the last day of April from the first day of May.

NANNO: April and May. The months of flowers. A Friday. The day consecrated to Venus. You were born under the junction of Venus and Phoebe. And it's Venus who dominates. It's she who makes you sweet, affable, given to love, prompt to devotion.

LUISA: I don't know if I am prompt in devotion, Nanno. But as for love, you are off. For I've never loved.

NANNO: You've never loved! And how old did you say? Twenty, right? But wait, wait!

LUISA: You are forgetting that I am married and that I love and respect my husband.

NANNO: I know that. But, I also know that this spouse is three times your age. You love him, but like a father. You respect him, but like an old man. Give me your hand. Here's the heart line. How it is stretched. Terrible sufferings. It breaks under them. Fatality! It traces in your white hand a line red like blood. Love passionate to violence.

LUISA: Don't I know better than anyone the degree to which my heart is calm?

NANNO: Wait, wait, I tell you. Incredulous one. The hour that is going to cause a great change in your destiny is about to strike. What funereal signs! Ah! (*she recoils*)

LUISA: Well, speak then.

NANNO: Don't ask me any more.

LUISA: You can speak. Go. I don't believe you. (*turning toward the right*)

NANNO: (*in a somber voice*) May science be deceived! May infallibility err!

LUISA: (*offering her hand with difficulty*) What do you see there?

NANNO: (*making an effort*) Well, I see you prisoner. I see you in danger of death.

LUISA: That's all?

NANNO: Isn't that enough?

MICHELE: (*leaning over Luisa's hand*) Why, Luisa bears the same sign as me.

NANNO: Shut up!

MICHELE: A cross in the middle of this line. You told me that means death on the scaffold.

NANNO: (*to Michele*) Shut up—wretch!

LUISA: And why should he shut up? Since you've begun to speak do so completely.

NANNO: We must not reveal the misfortunes that fate renders inevitable.

LUISA: (*revolting*) Inevitable! The scaffold for me?

MICHELE: Come on. One can avoid everything by taking care. Nanno, listen carefully to this. You must teach her this very minute where the danger is coming from or bad luck to you.

(*Nanno, without responding picks up her cloak from the ground, wraps herself in it and takes a step to withdraw. Michele grabs her hand.*)

MICHELE: You won't go like this.

NANNO: You both demand it. I will try to go further. If the evil can be conjured, we will conjure it. (*Nanno seems absorbed in contemplation.*)

LUISA: This danger where does it come from? And can you learn the cause?

NANNO: Love. Always. A fatal love. Irresistible. Mortal.

LUISA: But still, for whom? this love?

NANNO: For whom? Wait. I see him. Him. He's coming from far away, or rather coming back. He's crossing rivers and mountains. He's approaching. He's already breathing the same air as we do. Ah, he, too. A great danger threatens him. They're following him. They're spying on him. Under cloaks I see daggers gleam. (*exploding*) Ah, if he were killed—

LUISA: Well?

NANNO: If he were killed, you'd be saved.

LUISA: (*with spirit*) At that price, no! Let him bring me whatever fate wills. I won't pay for my safety with the life of another.

NANNO: (*moving slowly*) Then goodbye. Poor condemned woman. And may the decree of the stars be accomplished. (*she leaves*)

MICHELE: The plague chokes me! To have brought that Nanno. So I may be hanged. As for me, that's possible. I've got a bad head sometimes. And damn, when it comes to fighting, one puts one's hand in one's pocket and one finds a knife. The devil tempts you. The man falls. A bailiff arrests you. The judge condemns you. Master Donato slips the noose around your neck,—and you hang. Very well. But you, you, little sister. Who are you going to kill with your little hands. For in the end they only kill folks who've killed. And then here, no one kills the rich. Here, would you like to know what I say to you. From today, no longer speak of crazy Michele, but of Nanno the Madwoman.

LUISA: (*in a dull voice*) No, no. She sees what she spoke of.

SAN FELICE: (*who appears on Michele's last phrases*) What's the matter with you, Michele? *(to Luisa)* And who upset you?

MICHELE: Me, Excellency, who am only a dummy, and who deserves to be beaten.

LUISA: You've only obeyed me, Michele, don't reproach yourself. (*to her husband*) I will explain the enigma to you, my friend. You will laugh a little at me. That will do me good. Let's go inside. (*she takes her husband's hand and goes into the villa.*)

ANGIOLINA: Hanged. My poor Michele. So you seriously think you will be hanged.

MICHELE: For a moment. I will think a little on the day when I shall become Colonel.

(*They follow Luisa and her husband into the villa. Complete night. The clock of a neighboring church strikes eleven o'clock. Lady Hamilton enters wrapped in a cloak and a black mantilla. She wears a mask of black velour.*)

LADY HAMILTON: Eleven o'clock. The fountain of the Mergellina. This is it here.

CECILIA: Lord Nelson is going to be astonished.

LADY HAMILTON: The Queen will have deceived his impatience. Someone's coming. (*She goes behind the fountain with Cecilia.*)

SALVATO: Evidently they're following me. (*going to the left and noticing two bailiffs at the entry of a small street.*) And on this side they are barring my way. Here I am surrounded. This way, perhaps. (*goes to the right. Pasquale and his bailiffs appear.*) Again. There's no way, except to force a passage. (*going to the right*) Come. Make way.

PASQUALE: And if one doesn't make way for you. What would you say, my master?

SALVATO: I wouldn't say a thing. I would do something.

LADY HAMILTON: (*to Cecilia*) Why—I know that voice.

PASQUALE: Let's not get angry. Perhaps there's a way to understand each other.

SALVATO: It's my purse you'd have?

PASQUALE: Fie, signor. You have on you, I know it, a precious specimen of the writing of the illustrious General Championnet. Graciously cede this autograph to me and we will let you go.

SALVATO: And if I refuse?

PASQUALE: Alas, Excellency, you will put us to the sad necessity of killing you.

SALVATO: (*arming his pistols*) Then you'll need twenty rather than six, my knaves. An aide-de-camp of General Championnet is not so easily killed.

PASQUALE: Up to you, Beccaio. (*Salvato wraps his cloak around his arm, turns and fires to the right, then to the left. Two men fall. Then he draws his saber and leaps. He slaps his saber against the face of Beccaio who flees yelling, and with a blow of the tip of his saber rids himself of a fourth*) Damn! Four men knocked out. Why, he's a devil. He is going to escape us.

MAMMONE: Fear nothing. The French gentleman doesn't like one to approach him. We will fix him from a distance. (*hurling his knife*)

SALVATO: (*struck in the chest*) Ah! (*turns and falls at the door of the villa.*)

MAMMONE: His blood belongs to me. I will drink it to the last drop.

(*Pasquale and Mammone rush towards Salvato, but Lady Hamilton arises before them with a gesture to stop.*)

LADY HAMILTON: Go. The rest is my concern.

MAMMONE: Che pecora!

PASQUALE: (*grabbing him and dragging him away*) Shut up. The hand that pays has the right to command.

(*Mammone lets himself be pulled away, grumbling and swearing.*)

LADY HAMILTON: (*after watching them leave, leaning over Salvato*) I am afraid. The voice of this young man made me shiver. I cannot see his features. How thick the night is. (*the moon slips through some clouds. Lady Hamilton kneels anxiously and raises Salvato's fainted head. A ray of moonlight strikes his face. She jumps up abruptly letting his head fall*) Ah! Salvato! Salvato! The only being I've ever loved in this world, and it's I who've killed him!

CECILIA: Milady, mercy. Someone must have heard the noise of this struggle.

LADY HAMILTON: (*kneeling*) Salvato.

CECILIA: I see lights shining in that garden.

LADY HAMILTON: Yes, you're right. At this hour I don't have the right to weep. Marie Caroline would be jealous of my tears. The dispatches. (*she undoes his uniform and seizes a sealed dispatch case*.) I've got them.

(*Salvato revives, and seeing his dispatches in her hand, grabs her wrist, uttering a stifled cry. In the struggle her mask comes off.*)

SALVATO: The Lyonna. Ah, ah! Wretch! (*falling down after a vain effort to regain the papers. One of Lady Hamilton's bracelets remains in his shriveled hand.*)

LADY HAMILTON: (*dismayed*) Cecilia. He recognized me. Ah, come. Let's flee. (*they leave. Nanno comes forward slowly and leans over Salvato, then after examining him, resumes her full height.*)

NANNO: He's breathing. The fates are sealed. (*she rises and lets the door knocker fall twice, moves away a step, then extending her hand to the Villa San Felice*) Open, hospitable doors. The misfortune you are waiting for is here.

(*The door opens and Michele, a torch in hand rushes out followed by the Chevalier, Luisa and Angiolina. All peer at Salvato. The Curtain falls.*)

CURTAIN

ACT I

SCENE 2

The Banquet Hall of the Royal Palace. A large number of courtiers are present.

ACTON: (*in the midst of a group*) Yes, sir. The presence of the great Nelson ought to suffice to abort all the Jacobin conspiracies. The Revolution will recoil before this hero. Naples is saved.

KING: Ah! Ah! Lord Nelson doesn't waste time. He disembarked at five o'clock and he's saved us before midnight.

ACTON: That's the thought of Her Majesty, The Queen, that I am interpreting, Sire.

KING: Ah, very fine! Very fine! (*goes accompanied by Ruffo.*) What do you say about it, Cardinal? We've just completed enough pretty work and we are really prattling about it.

RUFFO: What you are doing, Sire, can never happen un-
noticed.

KING: Yes, that's the way you reassure us.

RUFFO: The hero of the Nile must suffice here, so long as
he's paid in advance. You made him Duke of Bronte,
joining an entailed estate to his commission of 15,000
pounds income; you've presented him with the sword of
Louis XIV, which comes to you from your grandfather,
Philip V of Spain. A beautiful weapon enriched with
diamonds that has the value of 125,000 pounds. You've
placed around his neck, the Order of Merit of Saint Ferdinand.

KING: By Jove, yes! I did all that. I slipped the ribbon
around his neck, gave him the sword, delivered the
commission. The Queen had decreed the thing thus.
But, indeed, I fear, between you and me, having committed a triple stupidity to humor him.

RUFFO: After all, what are you risking? A rupture with
France, no more.

KING: Wow! Nothing more than that! You are telling us a
pretty story.

MARIE CAROLINE: Milord Acton, do you think that
Nelson will follow us to the end?

ACTON: Your Majesty will do with him what she wishes.
She has an irresistible means of control over this plebe-
ian genius.

MARIE CAROLINE: What means?

ACTON: Love and ambition. Let Lady Hamilton decide and command in your name and Nelson will act.

MARIE CAROLINE: In that case, the subsidies—

ACTON: He has all the necessary power.

MARIE CAROLINE: As for General Mack?

ACTON: He's arming tonight in Naples, and will be incognito at my home ready to reveal himself at your first sign.

MARIE CAROLINE: Fine! You will convoke the Council for tomorrow at nine o'clock.

ADMIRAL CARACCIOLO: (*to Nicolino and Hector who arrive in court dress, but without powdered wigs*) Both of you here, after all that's happened. If the uproar of the sudden attack has reached the court—

HECTOR: They are already saying that the Procurator-Fiscal Vanni is disposed to put us on trial. Well, we are going to be ahead of him.

KING: (*to Cardinal Ruffo*) By the way, Cardinal, tell me, what's this Duchy of Bronte, I've just made a gift of to this Englishman? Bronte? Where's it located? In Calabria? In Sicily?

RUFFO: In the heart of Mount Etna, Sire.

KING: Huh? You say—?

RUFFO: The Queen, who is very learned—

KING: That's a fact. She knows everything.

RUFFO: Wanted to flatter, delicately—the vanity of Lord Nelson. She is very often reminded of the cyclops Bronte, spoken of in mythology, who in the crater of Mount Etna forged Jupiter's lightning.

KING: Perfect.

RUFFO: Then, in Greek, Bronte means thunder.

KING: Good. So, indeed, without suspecting it, I've created a Duke of Thunder.

NELSON: (*to Marie Caroline*) The hand of England soars over this cursed Revolution. William Pitt has sworn to choke it. Don't doubt, Madame, that he will keep his word. Everywhere that the French try to spread the fever of rebellion which excites it, we will always be there ahead of them, determined champions of the will of the Lord against the sons of Hell. Already, the task is more than half complete. France is exhausted of men, short of money, its best soldiers are shut up in Egypt with their most adept general. Believe me, it won't soon recover from the terrible blow our brave marines inflicted on it in the Bay of Aboukir.

MARIE CAROLINE: Ah, yes, France is uttering its death rattle. But we have to finish her off.

NICOLINO: Eh! Why we are here openly plotting.

(*Lady Hamilton enters through a door that opens behind the Queen.*)

MARIE CAROLINE: (*rising, going to her, clasping her hand*) Finally, there you are. The dispatches.

LADY HAMILTON: (*pointing to her breast*) I have it, here.

MARIE CAROLINE: How pale you are, my dear soul. Are you ill?

LADY HAMILTON: It's nothing. The sultry night air. A little emotion at the sight of the struggle.

MARIE CAROLINE: Ah! He defended himself.

LADY HAMILTON: (*bitterly*) And they killed him.

MARIE CAROLINE: (*with a gesture of indifference*) Come, you must be beautiful and smiling. Nelson is already ours if you will.

LADY HAMILTON: I will answer to you for him, Madame. Here he is.

(*Nelson comes forward and then goes with Lady Hamilton and the Queen to an alcove to talk. Vanni arrives; as he heads for the Queen, Nicolino and Hector confront him.*)

HECTOR: (*to Nicolino*) It's Vanni.

NICOLINO: (*bowing courteously but ironically to Vanni*) My word, Mr. Procurator-Fiscal. I am really ravished to see you.

VANNI: (*astonished, recoiling*) The Chevalier Caracciolo!

HECTOR: (*on the other side*) And as for me, I am no less enchanted to meet you.

VANNI: The Count de Ruvo!

NICOLINO: I've heard it often mentioned, your zeal to fulfill your duties. Some find you have too much of it.

VANNI: Chevalier.

HECTOR: As for your cleverness as a police official. It's legendary

VANNI: I am confused. (*aside*) What do they want coming here.

NICOLINO: Well, without any doubt, you have important news to announce to the court.

VANNI: Me—what?

NICOLINO: Why, for example that your agents have finally succeeded in putting their hands on the assassins of our unfortunate friend, Don Clemente.

(*The Queen, hearing these last words pronounced in a jesting way, rises and comes closer to hear better. The King suspends his conversation with Ruffo. Vanni who has recoiled a step, exchanges a glance with Marie Caroline. The group becomes the focus of all attention. All listen in silence.*)

VANNI: Alas, gentlemen, I am, on the contrary, distressed. Yes, it's like a thing done on purpose. I've ordered inquiry after inquiry.

NICOLINO: Well?

VANNI: All without success. The authors of this scandalous murder remain absolutely unfindable.

NICOLINO: (*more and more animated and bitter*) Even the head of the assassins, this Gaetano Mammone?

VANNI: (*faking astonishment*) Who is this? Mammone?

NICOLINO: Your agents ought to be able to inform you. But I pity your ignorance, Mr. Procurator-Fiscal. And I'm going to tell you so.

VANNI: You will oblige me greatly.

NICOLINO: Mammone is a flour dealer in the Vieux Marche. Your police can meet him every morning. He's a sort of ferocious beast who began one day when a barber was bleeding him by drinking the blood that was gushing out from his vein, and developing a taste for this terrible drink, killing to quench his thirst like a tiger.

VANNI: (*with coolness*) Very well. I see this. He's what we call a monomaniac.

NICOLINO: This monomaniac is at this hour, the terror of Naples. And by a strange privilege he circulates freely. It's true, they say, that Pasquale di Simone, one of your bailiffs, protects him.

MARIE CAROLINE: (*aside*) Insolent!

NICOLINO: This very day he had his designs on me. One moment I had him clinging to the end of my cane. And if he didn't have several dozen rascals of his own sort to defend him, I would have done my duty by dragging him with my own hand right to your office, Mr. Vanni, to procure you the advantage of cultivating his acquaintance.

VANNI: Ah—irritating turn of events, irritating.

NICOLINO: (*very hard and loud*) It's up to you to finish with this monster. Profit without further delay from the good advice I am giving you. His Majesty, The King, and Our Gracious Sovereign, who deign to hear me won't pardon you for leaving their faithful subjects precious existence to the mercies of this cannibal any longer.

ADMIRAL CARACCIOLO: (*coming forward*) Mr. Vanni.

VANNI: (*who was about to reply aggressively to Nicolino, bows low to the Admiral*) Milord!

ADMIRAL CARACCIOLO: My dear nephew is without doubt a little excited in his demeanor, but his advice is worth thinking on. Your responsibility is binding. Your duty is to take necessary measures to calm, without further delay, just concerns of the Neapolitan bourgeoisie. I am sure His Majesty won't contradict me.

RUFFO: (*low to the King*) Don't hesitate, sire. No solidarity with the dagger.

KING: (*to the Admiral*) My dear Admiral, you've spoken as a man of sense. I expect these disorders to cease. You understand me, Vanni, seize this Mammone for me and let them hang him.

(*Vanni, furious, bows and moves to the Queen.*)

VANNI: (*low to the Queen*) Madame, I had a crushing report against Nicolino. He maintained in public, before everyone, the most seditious language. I was going to unmask the Chevalier but the King imposed silence on me.

MARIE CAROLINE: Don't worry, Vanni. And don't expect anything to come of what's just happened. As for me, I do not fail to recognize your services and that ought to suffice for you.

VANNI: But Mammone?

MARIE CAROLINE: Leave him alone. The King won't remember tomorrow what he ordered tonight.

(*The doors at the back open revealing tables magnificently covered in an illuminated gallery.*)

MAJORDOMO: The Queen's supper.

(*The Queen like the King advances toward the Gallery. Acton offers her his hand. All follow. Nelson remains behind with Lady Hamilton.*)

NELSON: I belong to you body and soul. Must I burn this city which misjudges you, outrages you—tonight? From a look from your beautiful eyes I would set the fire with my own hand.

LADY HAMILTON: (*smiling*) The time hasn't come—yet.

(*They go in. An orchestra in the gallery at the back plays God Save The King. Universal acclamation. Hands extended to Nelson.*)

ALL: Long live Nelson! Long live the great Nelson!

(*At this moment the crowd separates in astonishment and fright. At the back, Citizen Garat, the French Ambassador appears in full dress. He takes two steps forward and stops. The entire assembly becomes mute. He leans on his saber which he holds in his left hand. A plumed tricolor hat is on his head.*)

NICOLINO: (*to Hector*) Garat. What's he come here to do?

GARAT: (*in a loud, firm voice*) Despite the ceaseless, repeated treasons of this lying court, I still doubted. I wanted to see with my own eyes, hear with my own ears. I've seen and I've heard. The Roman envoy brought to the Senate of Carthage in a fold in his toga either peace or war. As for me, I bring only war. For today, you yourselves have renounced peace.

ALL: (*the word runs like a murmur of fearful astonishment*) War!

NICOLINO: (*low to Hector*) War! Why then some misfortune has befallen Salvato. Wasn't he allowed to reach, Garat?

GARAT: (*continuing*) Thus, King Ferdinand; thus Queen Caroline. War, since you wish it. But this will be a war of extermination, I warn you of that. Despite the hero of this celebration, despite the impious power that he represents, war that will discard your throne and life. Goodbye! I am leaving Naples, the city of perjury. Close your gates behind me. Mass your soldiers on your walls. Erect your cannons on your fortresses. Assemble your fleets in your ports. You will make the vengeance of France slower, you won't make it less inevitable, nor less terrible! For all will give way before the shout of the great nation. Long live the Republic! (*Garat waives his hat, puts it on his head again, glares at the terrified and mute assembly, turns on his heel and leaves.*)

NICOLINO: (*to Hector*) The die is cast.

HECTOR: Let's hasten to warn our friends. (*They leave. At a sign from the Queen, the courtiers vanish, the doors are shut and only members of the Council remain on stage.*)

KING: (*very angry, pacing the stage and stopping to question various characters successively*) War! Now we are in fine shape! War! Eh! By Jove! Our good friend England has gained its ends. It's a question now of getting out of hot water! That's your affair, Mr. Acton.

MARIE CAROLINE: And that of the brave Nelson. Which ought to reassure you, Sire.

KING: Eh! Madame! War with the French is a weighty affair.

MARIE CAROLINE: You are forgetting that their thunder of war, their great conqueror, Citizen Bonaparte is locked up in Egypt.

KING: Yeah! But in default of Citizen Bonaparte there still remains France, Massena, the conqueror of Rivoli, Augereau, the victor of Lodi, Jourdan, the victor of Fleurus, and Moreau, and Brune. Which makes many conquerors for us—who've never conquered anything. Not counting Championnet, the victor of Dunes—who is only thirty leagues from us. That is to say a day's march.

MARIE CAROLINE: Oh! Championnet.

KING: It's not a question of shrugging one's shoulders, Madame. San Nicandro, my excellent preceptor vainly did his best to make an ass of me. I know enough to divine where you are leading us. It's no longer a question of sending to Toulon as was done in 1793, four vessels and 6,000 men. And they returned in nice condition, our ships and our men. It's no longer a question of furnishing to the coalition, as in 1796, our cavalry regiments to benevolently be hacked into mincemeat. It's a question of placing our troops in battle and to try our strength against the French. For your fine nephew, Francis of Austria is in no hurry to join our dance. As for him, he knows the French; he meddled with them and they drubbed him.

MARIE CAROLINE: But in the end, Sire, we had no choice.

KING: (*aside*) Hum! She's a sly one. (*aloud to Ariola*) Ariola, you pretend to have 65,000 men under arms. Where are they? Your 65,000 men!

ARIOLA: Why, Sire, there are 22,000 men in Camp San Germano; 16,000 in the plain of Sessa, 6,000 under the walls of Gaeta, 18,000 around Naples and the coasts. And 3,000 at Benevento.

KING: (*following the count on his fingers*) My word, he's got the count right. And I do have an army of 65,000 men.

ARIOLA: And all dressed to the nines in the Austrian fashion.

KING: That is to say in white.

ARIOLA: Yes, sire, instead of being dressed in green.

KING: Ah, my dear Ariola, dressed in white, dressed in green, go, they won't desert any less!

MARIE CAROLINE: Can you have such a sad opinion of your subjects, Sire—?

KING: As for me, madame, quite the contrary. I think my subjects are very intelligent. Too intelligent, even. And that's why I suspect they won't let themselves get killed for matters that don't concern them. What's it to them, if we stand well or ill with France? What's it bring to them to brave grape shot to assure us of victory? They would be very stupid. If I were a soldier in my service, the first day I would desert—with arms and equipment. And I would make myself a brigand. At least brigands fight and get killed for themselves.

MARIE CAROLINE: (*impatiently*) But, still—

KING: Still reliable or not we have an army. But a general? We must have a general.

MARIE CARLOINE: Sire, the case has been foreseen.

KING: Already!

MARIE CAROLINE: I asked my nephew to send us a man whose military reputation can impose on the enemy.

KING: And he found you this phoenix?

MARIE CAROLINE: Baron Charles Mack arrives tomorrow in Naples. Do you have something to say against him?

KING: Hum! I would have to say he's already been beaten by the French, but as this disgrace has occurred to all the generals of the Emperor including Prince Charles, his uncle, and your brother, I prefer Mack greatly to any other. So, we have an army and a general in chief; we lack only money. Look here, D'Ascoli, Ariola has counted his men for us. Count for us your shillings.

D'ASCOLI: Alas, the coffers of the Treasury—

KING: Are empty. I suspected that.

MARIE CAROLINE: Sire, you no more lack money than you do an army or a general. We have waiting at our disposition a million pounds sterling.

KING: Great! And who is the alchemist that has the happy faculty of making gold?

NELSON: Sire, I bear full powers of my government to treat with Your Majesty in the name of England, all questions relative to the war with France—

(*Meanwhile, the Queen goes to Lady Hamilton who gives her Salvato's dispatches. She breaks the seal, reads it, and manifests her joy with a gesture of triumph. Then she returns to the King, concealing the dispatch.*)

KING: (*low to Ruffo*) We are taken in a trap, Cardinal. You see; she's guessed and foreseen everything. (*aloud to Nelson*) But Your Grace has heard there's no money in our coffers.

NELSON: Sire, provision has been made. And Mr. Andre Backer, our banker who is here can affirm to you he's ready to pay in cash a letter of exchange for a million pounds which Sir William Hamilton will draw and I will endorse.

KING: (*walking*) It's very well managed; very well managed. Everything comes to hand and without need for me to wait. You will end by proving to me that the French have taken an oath to let themselves be beaten.

MARIE CAROLINE: Can Your Majesty be annoyed that fate has favored us? Must I still tell him that the French are in no condition to struggle against us.

KING: Huh? When they declare war—

MARIE CAROLINE: Citizen Garat was in too much of a
hurry. If he'd known the true situation in Rome he'd
have acted otherwise.

KING: Right! Right! Right! You know this before the
Ambassador.

MARIE CAROLINE: And would you believe General
Championnet himself?

KING: Huh?

MARIE CAROLINE: Read.

KING: (*casting a suspicious glance at the letter then passing it to Ruffo*) Read that to us, Cardinal.

RUFFO: (*reading*) My dear Garat, don't rush anything.
We must gain time at all costs. Our army at Rome
which amounts to 35,000 on paper, is in reality only
8,000, lacking shoes, clothes, and bread. I have hardly
100,000 cartridges to distribute. Our artillery is com-
posed of five cannons only. Our fortresses are as poorly
provisioned as our arsenals.

KING: (*enchanted*) Continue, Eminence, continue.

RUFFO: You understand, my dear Garat, that at this moment, I cannot repulse an attack, and have hardly any
ability to bring the war to Neapolitan territory.

KING: And this letter is really from Championnet?

RUFFO: (*with a touch of regret*) Yes, sire.

MARIE CAROLINE: (*to the King*) I hope that your concern is dissipated, sir?

KING: (*scratching his ear*) Why, without doubt, without doubt. (*at a sign from Ruffo he changes his tone*) Still, my good friend, England isn't giving its money for nothing. What does England demand in exchange for its money?

NELSON: A very simple thing which carries no prejudice to Your Majesty.

KING: Ah! Ah! And what is it?

NELSON: England asks that when the fleet of His Britannic Majesty, which is engaged in blockading Malta, shall have retaken it from France, The King of the Two Sicilies shall renounce asserting his rights over the island, so that England which has no possession in the Mediterranean other than Gibraltar, can make Malta into a station, a resupply point for its fleet.

KING: Right. Malta doesn't belong to me. It belongs to the order.

RUFFO: And if the Order is dissolved, Malta returns to the Crown of The Two Sicilies. Malta is worth more than a million pounds sterling.

KING: Surely, surely. (*day begins to dawn. Sounds of hunting can be heard*) The Tallyho! (*running to the window and opening it*) What's got into you sounding the Tallyho at dawn?

A HUNTSMAN: (*outside*) Your Majesty can leave when-
ever he wishes. The wild boars are started.

KING: Started. (*turning to his council*) You hear, the
boars are started.

HUNTSMAN: Yes, sire; a group of fifteen.

KING: Fifteen boars, by Jupiter. Fifteen boars. Gentlemen,
finish all your politics with the Queen. Fifteen boars.

RUFFO: And Malta, sire?

KING: Bah! Malta. I've not had it for 263 years, I can really do without it. A nasty rock which is only good for
hunting and migrant quail. Let them take Malta and rid
me of the Jacobins. Fifteen boars. Goodbye, gentlemen.
(*he leaves*)

MARIE CAROLINE: Milord, you can write to your government that the cession of Malta to England won't
cause any difficulties on the part of the King of The
Two Sicilies. Gentlemen; the Council is concluded. (*all
withdraw*)

MARIE CAROLINE: Finally, we are alone. And the game
is won, thanks to you, my dear soul. Thanks to that dispatch which allowed us to vanquish the King's reluc-
tance.

LADY HAMILTON: (*aside*) Alas, at what price?

MARIE CAROLINE: And that Cardinal Ruffo who was
pretending to dispute Malta with us—(*scratching at the*

small door on the right. Lady Hamilton goes to the door.)

LADY HAMILTON: It's Pasquale.

MARIE CAROLINE: Pasquale. Go open. (*Lady Hamilton opens*) You at this hour— What is there that's so serious?

PASQUALE: A strange thing, Madame. We've lost our cadaver.

MARIE CAROLINE: What? The Frenchman?

LADY HAMILTON: (*aside*) Salvato!

PASQUALE: When we returned to throw him into the gulf, he'd disappeared.

MARIE CAROLINE: Clumsy. To let him escape. You should have thought to kill him.

PASQUALE: There's some witchcraft, Madame, for Mammone's blows are sure. It's to give oneself to the devil and believe he was swallowed under ground.

MARIE CAROLINE: Where did this affair take place?

PASQUALE: Near the fountain of Mergellina, before the Villa San Felice.

MARIE CAROLINE: The Villa San Felice! Didn't you write a note affirming that the Chevalier had relations with I don't know what Jacobins?

PASQUALE: With Doctor Cyrillo. Yes, Madame. I've seen them myself leave the Chevalier's home in secret deliberations.

MARIE CAROLINE: (*to Lady Hamilton*) That's where he's hidden.

CURTAIN

ACT II

SCENE 3

The Garden of the Villa San Felice. To the left, the living quarters reached by a flight of stone steps from the garden. In the back a wall pierced by a small door giving on an alley. To the right, a large fig tree dominating a trellis which hides the wall from the park of the Duchess of Fusco. The garden contains ancient statues and vases from Pompeii. The vestibule of the house is decorated in Roman style, opening on galleries where the Chevalier San Felice, directed by the King to oversee the excavations at the foot of Mount Vesuvius, has provisionally assembled his precious discoveries. Table and chairs in front of the house.

At rise, Angiolina crosses the garden and heads toward the house, a box of flowers in her hand. Three knocks at the door in the wall. Angiolina goes to open it after a moment of hesitation, but soon wants to relock it from terror. Beccaio who appears doesn't give her time, jostling her and forcing his way in. As he rushes toward the steps, Angiolina screams.

ANGIOLINA: Help me! Help!

(*Michele appears at the top of the stairs, arms crossed. Beccaio, finding himself nose to nose with him is forced to back down the steps.*)

MICHELE: You are Beccaio who makes women scream.

BECCAIO: Let me pass.

MICHELE: Then it's not to pay court to Angiolina you are breaking down the doors. We were rivals in the past.

BECCAIO: I want to find the cursed dog who did this to me. (*pointing to the scar across his face*) He's here—

MICHELE: The Devil! Nice saber blow!

BECCAIO: One more time, let me pass. My Frenchman is hidden here.

MICHELE: Your Frenchman! You're dreaming! Your brain is damaged, poor fellow. And as for allowing you to enter—not at all. Your villainous face would frighten my sister, Luisa, too much.

BECCAIO: And I tell you that I intend to—

MICHELE: (*pulling his knife*) Take the measure of my knife. (*pushing him toward the back gate*) Look, it's just the shape of your wound. And if you don't get out of here right away, I'm going to complete Saint Andrew's cross on your bulldog face, Facchino! (*Beccaio decides to leave, but clearly showing he plans to return. The door locked, Michele turns to Angiolina.*) Nasty business! But hush! They're coming from the Duchess' garden.

(*They come through the arbor which leads to the home of the Duchess Fusco.*)

SALVATO: Oh! The doctor says I am quite healthy today.

CYRILLO: No imprudence! You must be patient for another week yet.

SAN FELICE: A fine cure, dear Cyrillo.

CYRILLO: Bah! Nanno did the best of it. These empiricists sometimes have marvelous cures. (*pointing to the arbor*) Then you are quite sure no one can suspect Salvato's presence?

SAN FELICE: In the Palace of Fusco? Everyone believes it uninhabited. This secret communication was known only to the Duchess and me. They can search my house. The Captain is safe there.

CYRILLO: Yes, they wouldn't dream of finding a door under this heavy arbor.

SAN FELICE: (*to Salvato*) We are forced to keep you in discomfort and to treat you a little like a prisoner, my dear Captain. But they have their eyes on us, and I would never forgive myself an imprudence that would place you in danger. (*to Cyrillo*) I am going to La Marinella.

CYRILLO: Me too.

SAN FELICE: (*as he leaves*) They are shipping me a whole convoy of figurines and amphora from Pompeii.

CYRILLO: You have marvels here.

SAN FELICE: The King's indifference to them leaves me free to enjoy them. (*they leave*)

LUISA: (*rejoining Salvato*) You are feeling better?

SALVATO: All my strength has returned. Cyrillo speaks like a doctor; but as for me, I must act like a man.

LUISA: (*placing her hand on her heart*) You wish to leave? To leave us?

SALVATO: It's necessary.

LUISA: Why, that's crazy. The least imprudence can place you in danger.

SALVATO: I've already delayed, too long. One day more consumed in cowardly inaction and I will be guilty. War's been declared. Neapolitan troops are marching on Rome.

LUISA: You know.

SALVATO: Pardon Michele. He told me everything.

LUISA: But the countryside is crawling with our soldiers. Think of it.

SALVATO: I am thinking of the dangers I am making you run through my presence.

LUISA: What chimeras!

SALVATO: You don't rescue with impunity folks that Marie Caroline has marked for her vengeance.

LUISA: Eh! What does that matter? To worry about that would mean to love mankind in a very cowardly way.

SALVATO: It's because I know your generosity, which nothing hinders, and will go to the point of sacrificing your life, that it is not permissible for me to put it to the test any further. What title have I to deserve this devotion? What am I to you! A passerby unknown the day before—forgotten tomorrow.

LUISA: (*aside, sadly*) Blind!

SALVATO: So long as my strength has betrayed my will, I abandoned myself. I became intoxicated by the sweetness of this angelic solicitude. But now I am on my feet; a sword is no longer too heavy for my hand. My decision is taken. I will leave this evening.

LUISA: (*sadly*) Leave then, since no word of a friend has the power to retain you. I am really forced to understand.

SALVATO: What do you mean?

LUISA: In my egoism, I was forgetting that perhaps some really dear friend awaits you with anxiety.

SALVATO: (*interrupting her*) What! Could you be thinking—?

LUISA: I have a restitution to make. As they brought you here, fainted, dying, your hand let a broken bracelet fall.

Doubtless some pledge of love that you wanted to press to your heart one last time.

SALVATO: (*astonished*) Me! A bracelet? Why, I'm unaware—

LUISA: (*giving him the bracelet*) Here it is. Perhaps, I've waited too long to return it to you.

SALVATO: (*remembering and understanding*) The coral bracelet. I was clutching it, did you say? (*as if suddenly struck by an idea*) Ah, I remember. (*explosively*) This— a pledge of love. Why, it's a witness to infamy.

LUISA: What do you mean?

SALVATO: I was alone when you found me on the square bathed in my own blood; and you were indeed unaware what had happened before your arrival. Struck by a dagger thrown from a distance, I'd fallen annihilated, paralyzed. Yet I still had feeling for things, and, as my assassins rushed on me, I saw standing at my side the shape of a woman, who, with a gesture, made them draw back. I can still hear, echoing in my ear, the phrase of the leader of the bandits, the hand that pays has the right to command. And they withdrew. The woman leaned over me. I could only see her eyes shining above her mask. She was masked. I felt her fumbling in my breast. It was my dispatches that she was stealing. Anger restored my strength. I tore myself from this woman, I grabbed her hand. In struggling against my grasp and fleeing, she broke her bracelet, and her mask fell off. This remained in my hand (*in a heavy voice*) and I recognized her.

LUISA: Then you know—?

SALVATO: (*bitterly*) Her name? Yes. But what does it matter? She cannot be made to pay for her crimes. All that I can tell you is she's not worth my hate. She is hardly worth my scorn. (*tossing the broken bracelet on the table.*) You see, no one regrets me. No one is waiting for me.

LUISA: (*aside, with a sigh of relief*) Ah!

SALVATO: And if I wish to leave—Ah, it's not because I wish to chase a lost love. It's because I wish to flee a love that is consuming me.

LUISA: Salvato!

SALVATO: Yes, the word's been said and there's no taking it back. I love you, Luisa. Your heart is so pure! Your soul so noble. How could I be able to resist the divine charm that you spread around you. Me, poor man disinherited of all joy, whose life up to this day is writhing in exile and in combat? Ah, yet this admission torn from the anguish of an inevitable separation, mustn't separate me from your esteem, Luisa. No bad thought, no guilty hope has germinated in this heart that belongs to you. I adore you. But as one who adores an angel in heaven, and I will take the memory of this ineffable virtue that nothing can tarnish, with me like a perfumed balm.

LUISA: (*shaking with emotion; grasping the chair near her*) Ah!

SALVATO: (*rushing to help her*) Luisa!

LUISA: (*stopping him with a gesture*) It's only joy. Ah, I am indeed happy! You are then such as I dreamed you to be!

SALVATO: What are you saying?

LUISA: I can speak in my turn. Each of us knows his duty and will put his glory to respect it. A chaste love for life is one that can be admitted with pride.

SALVATO: Oh darling Luisa!

LUISA: The generous friend that heaven has given me for a spouse has nothing to suspect in the affection that unites us. His honor is mine; it will always be precious to us. Isn't that true, my Salvato? The sisterly tenderness that I have for you cannot be lessened by the new feeling you've awakened in my heart. (*tenderly*) And now, my friend, are you still as determined to flee me?

SALVATO: Me—Great God!

LUISA: Who knows what the future holds for us. The hour of separation will always come too soon. Let's not run ahead of it.

SALVATO: My life, my will, my glory, Luisa, henceforth is to obey you. (*one can hear the bells sound, first in the distance, then closer and closer, from church to church.*) What's that?

LUISA: What can it mean? A religious celebration without doubt.

(*A cannon shot.*)

SALVATO: (*shaking*) That's the cannon. Something extraordinary is taking place in Naples.

LUISA: Ah, I was too happy.

(*Cannon and bells.*)

SALVATO: But we've got to know.

LUISA: Yes, yes. (*calling*) Angiolina, Michele! Angiolina! No one. (*the bells stop*) Ah, those bells. Wait, wait— (*going into the house*)

SALVATO: (*alone, listening*) The bells are silent. Was it really the cannon we heard? Our uneasy spirit took alarm too quickly. In Naples they like to make a racket over the least thing. Nothing more. (*returning to sit at the table*) Ah, Luisa loves me. What intoxication. I don't wish to think of anything but her. (*Uproar outside. He stands without leaving the bench to listen. Shouts and hurrahs come closer. On the other side of the wall rushing feet can be heard.*)

CROWD: (*outside*) Long live Nosey! Long live General Mack! Death to the Jacobins! Death to the French. (*the bells begin to ring again. Salvato turns toward the back and sees Nanno entering slowly and silently.*)

SALVATO: Nanno! Hello, Mother. I thank you for coming to see your patient.

NANNO: It's the cured soldier I've come to see. While he abandons himself to the intoxication of love, blood is spilling down there.

SALVATO: (*jumping up*) They're fighting, right? Those bells, those shouts, that cannon which is growling again—are announcing some Neapolitan victory over the French. Where are they fighting, Nanno?

NANNO: Ferdinand has entered Rome, and the massacres have begun. They are cutting the throats of the friends of France, or shooting the sons of liberty. They are burning the Jews. Your general needs all his swords. Your place in the great battle which is going to be offered is conspicuous. Don't delay your share of the combat for an hour, or the glory will be taken and shame will install itself in your bed.

SALVATO: Thanks, Nanno. No one will take my role in danger. But why are you coming to urge me to combat? You, a subject of King Ferdinand?

NANNO: Nanno is not Neapolitan. Nanno is the daughter of Albania and the Albanians fled their country so as not to be anybody's subject. All people who rise up in the name of liberty are our brothers. And Nanno prays the Panagie to protect the French who are fighting for the liberty of nations. (*Michele moves the arbor communicating with the villa of the Duchess of Fusco, and goes to Salvato.*)

SALVATO: (*noticing Michele*) Ah! Michele. Tonight I must be far from Naples.

MICHELE: Everything is prepared. A costume like mine awaits you here. You can speak the Napelese dialect like a true lazzaroni. You will pass through the gates without hindrance. And be safe on the road to Capua.

Towards dusk we will find Pietro with a horse who will do his thirty leagues without getting winded.

SALVATO: Come on, then. (*aside, stopping*) But Luisa.

NANNO: (*pointing to the house*) Be careful what you are going to do. If you leave without turning your head you can spare her a cruel death.

SALVATO: What are you saying there?

NANNO: The moment is solemn. Your love condemns her.

SALVATO: What madness!

NANNO: Your abandonment will save her. When you've crossed that sill, (*pointing to the door leading to the Duchess villa*) if you return on your path, poor children, you are both lost. Goodbye, I've spoken. My mission is accomplished. (*She leaves.*)

SALVATO: Leave! Without seeing her again. Renounce her forever. Is this possible? Ah, come Michele. (*he flees distracted, at the moment Angiolina enters. The arbor closes. Luisa appears on the steps.*)

LUISA: (*rushing down the stairs to Angiolina*) Salvato?

ANGIOLINA: (*pointing to the arbor*) He went with Michele. In a quarter of an hour they will be out of Naples.

LUISA: (*rushing*) He's leaving. I must speak to him.

ANGIOLINA: (*with a gesture of fright*) Don't go, Signora.

LUISA: (*astonished*) What's the matter with you?

ANGIOLINA: The Queen is right behind me.

LUISA: (*shocked*) The Queen!

ANGIOLINA: The Chevalier has arrived back unexpectedly. Just in time to receive her.

LUISA: What's she coming to find here?

(*The Queen enters with the Chevalier and Lady Hamilton.*)

QUEEN: (*to the Chevalier*) I've thought of surprising you this way for a long while, chevalier. And I warn you I won't be satisfied with a single figurine.

SAN FELICE: Many times I've begged the King—

QUEEN: Good! If you wait for the King to find time to take account of your scientific investigations you will lose your glory. They say marvelous things about your collections. Amongst others, don't you have a bust of Tiberius, and a Mercury with a caduceus?

SAN FELICE: In a perfect state of preservation. Your Majesty shall judge—

QUEEN: Come on, show me the way.

(The Chevalier offers his arm to the Queen and takes her up the stairs. The lords of the suite accompany them. Lady Hamilton remains behind and pulls Luisa aside.)

LADY HAMILTON: *(very excited)* Listen to me!

LUISA: *(astonished)* Milady?

LADY HAMILTON: Perhaps you've already guessed this visit to the Chevalier's collections is only a pretext on the part of the Queen.

LUISA: What do you mean?

LADY HAMILTON: You are accused of hiding a proscribed— The Procurator-Fiscal is entering at this moment by way of the quay?

LUISA: *(distracted)* Vanni!

LADY HAMILTON: I am counting on you to help me save the one you are hiding.

LUISA: You!

LADY HAMILTON: I came for that.

LUISA: *(aside)* If this is a trap. *(aloud)* I don't understand.

LADY HAMILTON: I beg you, let's not play at cross purposes. This is not the moment. This seems strange to you; unreal, impossible—that I, the friend and confidant of the Queen, am going against her designs. Well, that's still so, and you must believe me.

LUISA: But, Milady—

LADY HAMILTON: To convince you is it necessary that I push frankness to the limits? So be it. The man they are pursuing, that they are searching for, it's death if they catch him. I loved that man madly. I still love him.

LUISA: (*taken aback*) Oh!

LADY HAMILTON: And I don't want him to die, you understand?

LUISA: (*aside, with horror*) Salvato, the lover of this woman!

LADY HAMILTON: (*looking at the interior of the house*) Look, I beg you, there's not a minute to lose. The Queen is still there. Vanni, before acting, must present himself to the Chevalier. Make Salvato come. The officers of the escort who are posted outside will protect his flight. It's agreed. I've deliberately kept away the bailiffs who know him and Vanni has never seen him.

LUISA: (*aside, allowing herself to fall onto a bench*) The lover of this woman. It seems to me everything is crumbling around me.

LADY HAMILTON: (*coming to Luisa*) Well? You don't answer. What are you thinking of? Time is wasting.

LUISA: I don't know the man of whom you are speaking.

LADY HAMILTON: You don't know him, you haven't hidden him, nursed him. (*noticing the bracelet left by*

Salvato on the table) Ah! Why, you are lying. He's here. For this bracelet. (*she stops*)

LUISA: (*looking and seeing the like bracelet on her, she rushes and grasps her wrist*) Ah! The same. (*pushing Lady Hamilton's arm away violently*) Ah, the wretch! She says she wants to save him and she's the one who had him assassinated to steal from him.

LADY HAMILTON: (*drawing back so she is concealed by the pedestal from Salvato who enters*) Ah!

LUISA: Her pity was a trick. She was hoping in this way to find the one she pursued with her hate. But the snare was too obvious, Madame. As if Salvato, that generous and noble heart, would ever be able to forget himself to the degree of loving such a creature!

LADY HAMILTON: Take care!

LUISA: They've boasted to me about your talent as an actress, Lady Hamilton. I thank you for having given me a sample of your ability; but don't waste any more time in this role to no purpose. At this time, Salvato is in safety far from Naples, far from here, and sheltered from the daggers of your bailiffs!

LADY HAMILTON: You are mistaken madame, for there he is!

LUISA: (*turning*) Great God.

SALVATO: (*bewildered, stepping back*) The Lyonna! Fool that I am! Nanno spoke truly.

LADY HAMILTON: (*aside*) Salvato is her lover. Bad luck to her!

(*The Queen and her suite enter with San Felice and Vanni.*)

QUEEN: (*to San Felice*) You must excuse Vanni, my dear Chevalier. He cast himself on a false track, I was certain of it. I knew in advance he wouldn't find anything to suspect. But you see, to confound him, the best thing is to let him do it.

SAN FELICE: The Procurator-Fiscal can act with complete freedom. I don't see any objection. (*at this moment, he notices Salvato who, fixed by the glance of Lady Hamilton has remained motionless near a large Pompeian vase on a marble pedestal, aside*) God! The imprudent!

LADY HAMILTON: (*advancing towards the Queen*) The most curious pieces of the Chevalier's collection are not in the gallery, Madame. Take the trouble to look over here. What you see will be worth an attentive examination.

LUISA: (*collapsing on a bench*) He's lost.

QUEEN: Let's see. What do you have to show me that's so marvelous?

LADY HAMILTON: (*leading the Queen past Salvato*) Why—this vase.

QUEEN: (*aside, looking at Lady Hamilton*) What a singular smile. (*aloud*) Indeed, this vase is admirable. (*aside*) Who is this young man? (*aloud*) Who are you?

SAN FELICE: (*advancing*) Madame, that's Michele, the Lazzaroni, Michele, the Mad. The milk brother of Signora San Felice, my wife. (*Michele appears in the opening of the arbor without being seen.*)

MICHELE: Huh?

QUEEN: Ah, really. (*aside*) That smile persists. (*aloud*) The milk brother of the Signora. (*to Lady Hamilton*) You spoke the truth, my sweet. This vase is a masterpiece. Chevalier, you must sacrifice it to me.

SAN FELICE: Why, this vase belongs to Your Majesty.

QUEEN: In that case, I'm taking it away. Place that vase on your shoulder, my lad. In a moment we will put it in my carriage. (*Salvato bows*)

LADY HAMILTON: (*passing close to Luisa, low*) Don't be afraid for him. It's not Salvato, Madame, who must pay me for your outrages. (*While Lady Hamilton is near Luisa, Michele slides near Salvato as he is about to pick up the vase. He pushes Salvato behind the statue towards the arbor and takes the vase in a way so his face is concealed.*)

MICHELE: (*low to Salvato*) Go back in, quickly. I'll answer for everything. (*Salvato vanishes behind the arbor. None of the characters notice the substitution.*)

QUEEN: (*To Vanni, who comes down the steps followed by some police officers*) Well, Mr. Procurator-Fiscal, here you are back, empty handed; I can see from your face. I predicted it to you, but you are the most obstinate man.

VANNI: When it's a question of service to Your Majesty.

QUEEN: (*low*) As for me, I've found him.

VANNI: (*low*) Here?

QUEEN: You see that Lazzaroni carrying a vase on his shoulder?

VANNI: Yes.

QUEEN: That's our man disguised. Some of your men know this Salvato?

VANNI: Yes. Pasquale. Beccaio.

QUEEN: Warn them. And if it's really him—

VANNI: To Fort Saint Elmo with him.

QUEEN: (*aloud*) Don't forget, Mr. Vanni, that you owe excuses to the Chevalier—

SAN FELICE: Oh, madame, I dispense with them willingly, Mr. Procurator-Fiscal.

QUEEN: Then it's up to me to repair his wrongs, and so no one will doubt our favor remains secure, I am taking you to the Palace, Chevalier.

SAN FELICE: Madame.

QUEEN: I must consult your taste on where to place this beautiful vase. Come on. (*The Chevalier bows and follows her. At Vanni's direction, Pasquale and Beccaio have come. Lady Hamilton leaves with the Queen without noticing them. Michele amuses himself by hiding his face from Pasquale and Beccaio who try to peep at him, as if he was afraid of being recognized. Then, when they get close to him, he abruptly places the vase on the ground mopping sweat from his face.*)

MICHELE: By Saint Janvier. How heavy that devilish pot is.

LUISA: (*in a choked voice*) It's Michele.

PASQUALE and BECCAIO: (*stupefied*) Michele, the Fool!

MICHELE: Well, yes. Michele. Delighted to see you so as to turn the drudgery over to you. (*placing the vase in the bewildered hands of Pasquale*)

PASQUALE: Hey! What the Hell am I supposed to do with this?

MICHELE: Carry it to the carriage, and quickly. The Queen's waiting. (*pushing them toward the back, they disappear*) Oof! We had a close call! (*looks and listens at the back. Angiolina returns to Luisa.*)

MICHELE: (*posting himself near the house so he can see what's going on outside*) Pasquale's putting the vase down. He's explaining to Vanni that I am really myself,

Michele, the Fool, and no one else. What a crestfallen look. The Queen understood his look. She's pale, too. The carriage is leaving, the escort follows. (*raising his voice*) Bonifaccio! Lock the gate with a triple lock. And don't open to a living soul. (*going to Luisa*) Little sister!

LUISA: (*very absorbed, eyes fixed*) It's you, Michele.

MICHELE: In less than a quarter of an hour it's necessary that the Captain and I leave by the gate to Capua.

LUISA: (*shaking her head*) Oh—oh. Yes. You must.

MICHELE: Vanni and his consorts might have a second thought and return on their tracks.

LUISA: It's true.

MICHELE: I'm going to assure myself that they haven't planted spies around the villa and in the alleyways. Meanwhile, say your goodbyes because as soon as I return, I'm carrying him off.

LUISA: (*to herself*) She recognized him. With a word she could have given him away. Why is it she didn't denounce him? Could it really be true she loves him? And him? (*Michele goes to find Salvato. Then he leaves by the small door. Angiolina watches out the back. Salvato approaches Luisa and kneels. Night slowly comes on.*)

SALVATO: Ah! Luisa. I am a wretch, accursed. I ought to have fled without trying to see you again. Will you forgive me for ruining your calm? All this hate that I've just unchained against you?

LUISA: (*slowly looking in his eyes*) Above everything, I've sacrificed my life to our love. It's not for that, Salvato, that you need my pardon.

SALVATO: (*astonished*) Why, for what then?

LUISA: Is it really possible you lied to me?

SALVATO: Me?

LUISA: That woman loves you. That woman pretends to have rights over your heart.

SALVATO: (*rising with a gesture of disgust*) The Lyonna!

LUISA: Just now your life was at her discretion. Isn't her generosity proof of her love?

SALVATO: (*indignant*) Her generosity is an offense. Her love was defiling. Luisa, don't you know who that woman is? Born in the mud of London she went from tavern to tavern selling her charms. Her beauty is justly celebrated in that city for she has no mysteries about her person. And when Lord Hamilton married her and made her a peeress of England he was congratulated, facetiously, for having legitimized the type of amorous fantasies of his colleagues in the Upper Chamber! A day came, when this grand priestess of vice wanted to satisfy a caprice. She gave walking papers to her favorites for a while; stripped off her infamous luxury, hid under an assumed name her notorious celebrity. That way, she hoped to abuse the ignorance and credulity of a Proscribed. By luck, an honest, indignant man was found in time to tear off the veil in which she had wrapped herself. And he who was, perhaps, destined to become the dupe of this false innocent fled with horror and disgust from the prostitute clinging to his knees. That's the truth, Luisa. The poison had been poured, the champagne glass held out, but my lips never touched it, I swear to you.

LUISA: (*falling into his arms*) O my Salvato! What a weight you've taken from my heart. How happy I am!

SALVATO: My friend!

MICHELE: (*rushing in*) Come on, Captain. Presto! The road's clear.

LUISA: Yes, leave. You must. Till we meet again, friend. May the Lord and his angels guard you.

SALVATO: Till we meet again. But don't you know there will be a danger of death for you if we ever see each other again.

LUISA: (*tenderly hushing his mouth with her hand*) Shut up! Let's place the unknown things of the future in God's hands. But whatever happens, I will never leave you on the word goodbye.

SALVATO: Well, so be it. Dear darling of my heart. Till we meet again.

MICHELE: Listen—

FISHERMEN: (*outside, singing*)
Fisherman, the tide sleeps
And the wind's easing off.

What are you looking for in the port?
It's the Tarentine
Alone in the night.
See the graceful girl
With beautiful eyes
Follow your shining lantern.

MICHELE: Those are the fishermen of Marinella who are going to cast their nets in Pausilippa.

SALVATO: We must let them move away.

MICHELE: Not at all. Heaven favors us. They are all comrades, I can answer for. In their company you have nothing to worry about.

SALVATO: (*to Luisa*) Till we meet again!

LUISA: Oh! yes. To see you again. At the price of my life.

CHORUS:
Fisherman, the tide sleeps
And the wind's easing off.
What are you looking for in the port?
It's the Tarentine
Alone in the night.
See the graceful girl
With beautiful eyes
Follow your shining lantern.

CURTAIN

ACT III

SCENE 4

The Castle at Caserta. A circular reception hall giving on the right to the apartments of the Queen. To the back, a peristyle with a triple staircase. To the right doubled hinged windows communicating with a vast terrace. Beyond this terrace can be seen in profile a portico supported by 64 noble columns and the trees of the park. Moonlight outside. Candelabras and lit chandeliers. Lady Hamilton is seated at a table to the right going through some papers. Vanni enters and going to her, begins to speak. At his first words she rolls up the papers, smiling with a cruel smile, as if enjoying in advance what she is preparing. To the left the doors are open and people can be seen talking and circulating.

VANNI: Is it possible, Milady, that the Queen has pardoned this San Felice?

LADY HAMILTON: What makes you believe that?

VANNI: They told me that she's here, at Caserta. She tricked us, Milady. Salvato Palmieri really was hidden by her.

LADY HAMILTON: We know that—

VANNI: And they haven't yet ordered me to find his accomplices.

LADY HAMILTON: We know them.

VANNI: (*surprised*) They investigated the affair without me?

LADY HAMILTON: Don't worry, Mr. Procurator-Fiscal, this very evening Her Majesty will give you her instructions.

VANNI: Then I can put my hand—

LADY HAMILTON: On all the leading Jacobins in Naples.

VANNI: And this time, they'll let me use the extraordinary methods—

LADY HAMILTON: You shall act with complete freedom.

VANNI: Even with respect to La San Felice?

LADY HAMILTON: Oh, as to her. The Queen and I will be responsible for her punishment.

VANNI: Are you afraid I will spare her because she's a woman? A criminal has no sex to me. We will begin with the boots. A few wedges applied will suffice to extract a confession.

LADY HAMILTON: (*smiling*) I have something better than that.

VANNI: (*astonished*) I will apply the strapado. Hands behind the back, the condemned is suspended like a chicken.

LADY HAMILTON: I've got better than that.

VANNI: I understand. You prefer the iron cap which disfigures?

LADY HAMILTON: I've got better than that, I tell you. With such a woman one must strike her through her heart. I will leave her life. But I will dishonor her; I will make her an object of scorn and disgust for all those who venerate her, all those who love her. I want them to believe they are perishing at her hands. Delivered and sold by her. Let them all walk to the scaffold renouncing her and cursing her. Let her know, and be unable to wash away this stain. I want her to die of her own rage; of her own despair, of her own shame; fully convinced that her name will remain infamous and her memory forever execrated.

VANNI: There's nothing for me to do but bow, Milady. I could never have invented that.

LADY HAMILTON: Come to the Queen's. (*they go into the Queen's apartment and disappear. Fragola, dressed as a page enters, looking for someone.*)

FRAGOLA: Where can the Signora be? (*observing Luisa enter followed by a Duenna*) Ah! (*rushes to her then stops*) That cursed Duenna again. Right; a duenna; ought to be a food fancier. (*leaving by the right. The doors at the back are closed.*)

DUENNA: Your ladyship is not going to supper with the Queen?

LUISA: No, I am ill. But you are free, Euphrasie.

DUENNA: Not at all, Signora. My mission is to carry the fan, the handkerchief and the bonbons. I cannot distance myself.

LUISA: But I never use kerchiefs, nor sweets. You know that quite well.

DUENNA: That doesn't matter, Signora. (*Luisa sits; the Duenna sits ten paces away.*)

LUISA: (*rising impatiently*) Ah! (*she heads towards the terrace*) I need some air.

(*The Duenna follows her. At the moment she sets foot on the terrace a guard appears and bars her passage.*)

GUARD: No one can pass.

DUENNA: Access to the terrace is forbidden at this time.

LUISA: Spied on, isolated, a prisoner.

(*Two lackeys open the double doors to the great staircase and stand aside to let Admiral Caracciolo pass.*)

LUISA: The Admiral. (*rushing to him*) Oh, my dear prince, how happy I am to see you. You, at Caserta?

CARACCIOLO: Yes, I am so ill at court that this must appear strange to you, my dear child. (*The Duenna approaches to listen. Caracciolo glares at her and she steps back.*)

DUENNA: Oh, my sweet Jesus. What a look! (*she remains at a distance*)

CARRACCIOLO: But I've come to insist on an explanation from Mr. Acton about an incredible order given in my absence.

LUISA: Which is?

CARACCIOLO: I've spent twenty-four hours in Gaeta, and they profited by it to bring ashore all my stores from the fleet and consigned my marines to the Chateau de l'Œuf!

LUISA: Some machination of Lord Nelson.

CARACCIOLO: That man will cost Naples dear. But you, Luisa. You've resumed your functions near the Queen.

LUISA: Yes, after two years of indifference, she's remembered that I belong to her house. But beware of believing from this that I am in favor.

CARACCIOLIO: What do you mean?

LUISA: I had the misfortune of being an obstacle to the Queen's vengeance. I committed the unforgivable crime of penetrating the secrets of Lady Hamilton and I am here the prisoner of their combined hate. For fifteen long days they've kept the Chevalier away and I feel myself entangled in I don't know what dark intrigue. And I struggle in vain under the hypocritical caresses of these two women who are working mysteriously to engrave on my heart a revenge worthy of their atrocious geniuses.

CARACCIOLO: Beware.

LUISA: My dear, prince. In a situation where life and honor are engaged you have to look your adversaries in the face. Leave me then the joy of letting them know my pride defies their threats and my courage will defy their tortures.

CARACCIOLO: Then it's open war.

LUISA: Under the cover of the most perfect courtesy. We exchange compliments which are bitingly savage. If the blow which must strike me hasn't fallen yet, ah, it's not for failing to provoke it.

CARACCIOLO: (*astonished*) Such an over excitement—

LUISA: Ah, it's what you don't know, my friend. What fever of revolt they succeeded in vivifying here. For the small thing of having a high heart and an honest soul! But all that I respect, all that I admire, is every day the object of filthy sarcasms from this pack of fawning courtiers.

CARACCIOLO: Yes—

LUISA: Why, there's not a generous feeling they don't attempt to travesty. Not a shining truth fails to serve as the butt of their cynical jeers.

CARACIOLO: It's true.

LUISA: Inept slanders, stupid inventions, perfidious subtleties, all is good for them to drag into the mud under the eyes of Marie Caroline. Our purest virtues and our most cherished glories. Must they flatter her ferocious hates and justify her thirst for tortures!

CARACCIOLO: Infamy—

LUISA: It's on the advice of these wretches that she left Naples. They made her hope that by leaving the field by her absence to the Neapolitan patriots, they would rush into some imprudent undertaking.

CARACCIOLO: Yes, yes. That must be it.

LUISA: Ah, tell them indeed to be mistrustful. That massacres are being prepared, and scaffolds ordered. Ah, let them be patient for the hour is approaching when the collapse will come by itself. When we will see this mad tyranny commit suicide by its own hands.

CARACCIOLIO: While waiting, they are placarding all the street corners with bulletins of General Mack's victories.

LUISA: Do you believe these Austrian fantasies? Mack making Championnet flee? All this will end in some lightning blow which will pulverize their triumphal arches. As for what will become of me in the midst of this tempest, I am unaware. (*she offers him her hand which he takes in his and shakes.*) But this is a consolation to me. At this grave hour of my life to be able to shake your hand. You will bear me witness, if I must be conquered in this struggle. You can tell friends separated from me that I've fallen worthy of them.

CARACCIOLO: (*with emotion*) I give you my word for that, generous child!

AN USHER: His Excellency, the Captain General attends the Lord Admiral in the Council Chamber.

(*Caracciolo makes a gesture of farewell and leaves. Fragola enters with a plate covered with cups and fruits, offering some to the Duenna.*)

FRAGOLA: Iced oranges, noble lady. Marzipan.

DUENNA: (*ravished*) Oh. Great idea. Oh, what a nice young man! (*she takes from the plate several times, spreading it all in her handkerchief on the table at the right.*)

FRAGOLA: (*smiling*) Take more of these candied citrons.

DUENNA: Why, yes. Really, yes. The pretty cherub is right.

FRAGOLA: (*aside*) Good. Now she's provided for. A famished stomach has no ears. (*approaching Luisa*) A cup of Spanish chocolate, Signora?

LUISA: (*without looking at him*) Thanks.

FRAGOLA: (*low*) Mercy. Pretend to take some. I have to talk to you.

LUISA: (*turning*) Huh?

FRAGOLA: (*watching the Duenna out of the corner of her eye*) I am Fragola the little shop keeper.

LUISA: (*recognizing her*) Why, yes.

FRAGOLA: It's Doctor Cyrillo who sent me.

LUISA: In this costume.

FRAGOLA: It was really needed to get into Caserta. The doctor and his friends received a letter from you two days ago.

LUISA: From me?

FRAGOLA: At least it appears so from the signature. The letter contains a single phrase.

LUISA: Hurry up.

FRAGOLA: In the name of the absent let each of the brothers appear next Friday midnight at the home of the Duchess Fusco. Urgent communication from the general.

LUISA: And signed by me?

FRAGOLA: The doctor fears some trap.

LUISA: It is one.

FRAGOLA: And what confirms them in this idea is that they found the cadaver of Pagacella on the road from Villetri.

LUISA: Salvato's messenger.

FRAGOLA: Stripped of his dispatches.

LUISA: Thanks to the captured papers they will have plotted some betrayal.

FRAGOLA: Then no one should come to the rendezvous.

LUISA: Let them be very careful. It's Vanni and his Bailiffs they will find there. (*the doors open, Fragola escapes.*)

AN USHER: The Queen's amusements.

MARIE CAROLINE: (*entering*) What pretty darling, alone here? (*looking around her*) With Donna Euphemia. (*caressing her hair*) This pretty head. Is it still solid?

LUISA: Your goodness confuses me. I have my head about me, I assure you. For the moment at least.

MARIE CAROLINE: So much the better, dear child, and may that continue! (*as these words are spoken the lack-*

eys and majordomos have set up two card tables. That of the Queen to the right and that of the ladies in waiting to the left. Luisa, after having bowed to the Queen goes to the table at the right.)

VANNI: (*approaching the Queen*) I take my leave of Your Majesty.

MARIE CAROLINE: Yes. Listen Vanni and execute my instructions. (*low*) Don't leave Caserta. Go to my office and await my instructions. The dictated letter will be brought to you by Lady Hamilton. (*Vanni bows and leaves.*)

ACTON: (*to Caracciolo*) Your marines are rough soldiers. We want to use their energy by confiding to them our advanced posts. 1,500 to 2,000 will be chosen for this service. The rest will be returned to you.

CARCCIOLO: Then tomorrow.

ACTON: Tomorrow everything will be settled.

CARACCIOLO: (*looking at Luisa, aside*) Her equivocal smile seems the negation of his promises.

LADY HAMILTON: (*to Nelson*) Dear Horatio. Where does this somber, preoccupied face come from?

NELSON: I am always preoccupied when action is underway.

LADY HAMILTON: Do you doubt General Mack?

NELSON: All battles are doubtful.

LADY HAMILTON: But, still—

NELSON: If Mack is beaten, the French will be in Naples in three days.

MARIE CAROLINE: Milord, do you esteem our soldiers so little that you can think the Republicans can conquer when outnumbered six to one. Those you attack with your English in equal and often in inferior numbers.

NELSON: On the sea, yes. Because the sea is our element. It belongs to the English. But on land it's another matter. God knows I hate the French. I've vowed a war of extermination against them. But detesting one's enemy is no reason not to do him justice. Who says hate doesn't say scorn. If I scorned the French I wouldn't give myself the trouble of hating them.

A MAJORDOMO: (*introducing a courier*) A message from His Majesty.

MARIE CAROLINE: (*seizing the letter presented by the courier*) A letter from the King. Ah! Milord, I hope we are going to find here what will give the lie to your irritating prognostications.

NELSON: I am the first to wish it, Madame.

MARIE CAROLINE: (*reading*) Madame, and dear spouse. This morning, General Mack and I, your servant, left together to hunt stags at Corneto; General Mack to course the French from Civita-Castellana. All during my hunt I heard cannon which didn't fail to rejoice me. The republicans lack artillery. I am writing you to kill time, dinner being late. This evening, I am going to the theatre where I will show these clumsy Romans how to eat macaroni in the Neapolitan way. On that subject, I pray to God he keeps you in his holy and worthy care—Ferdinand.

ANDRE BACKER: All day under Mack's cannon fire. Why the Republicans must be annihilated.

MARIE CAROLINE: There's a post script. As soon as I've received from Mack the bulletin detailing the victory, I will send it to you by a new courier, who will also bring you the flags that our brave Neapolitans have taken away from the French.

ANDRE BACKER: Admirable. Now that's what's called talking like a king.

CARACCIOLO: (*low*) A King Nosey.

ACTON: (*who's been questioning the courier and has received other dispatches*) The dispatches sent me by General Ariola confirm this excellent news.

MARIE CAROLINE: Ah!

ACTON: The French are in full retreat. An enemy who wants to avoid combat defends himself ill. Mack's cannon, doubtless, announced he has changed their retreat into a route.

MARIE CAROLINE: So—we are masters of the Roman states.

ACTON: Yes, Madame. But our victory in Civita-Castellana must have an echo in the Rue Toledo. The

Jacobin Rebellion was becoming threatening. It's necessary to finish with it. (*with a sign of intelligence addressed to the Queen*) A note intercepted by Ariola. (*showing a paper.*)

MARIE CAROLINE: (*taking the paper*) Let's see, let's see.

ACTON: And if the Procurator-Fiscal is not to lose a minute—

MARIE CAROLINE: (*still reading*) But he's left Caserta.

ACTON: It's necessary to have someone run after him. Or write to him.

MARIE CAROLINE: Write to him. And right away. You are right. (*goes to the table where Luisa has been speaking low to Caracciolo and, as if by chance, offers Luisa a pen from the table.*) Write, dear little one. I am going to dictate.

LUISA: (*astonished, frowning, takes the pen*) I am waiting, Madame.

MARIE CAROLINE: Mr. Procurator-Fiscal. I've already made known to you the names of the principal conspirators.

LUISA: (*aside*) Ah, I understand. (*writing rapidly, aloud*) It's written, madame.

MARIE CAROLINE: At this time I can give you with certainty the place, the day and the time of their next rendezvous.

LUISA: (*calmly*) Next rendezvous. (*writes rapidly, aside*) I wasn't mistaken.

MARIE CAROLINE: It's for midnight tomorrow. All the heads of the party will meet at the home of the Duchess Fusco. The password is Rome and Naples.

LUISA: Is that all?

MARIE CAROLINE: (*appearing to hesitate*) Good. Add: You know all you can want me to tell you. (*she watches Luisa write, extending her hand for the paper.*) That's finished. Give it to me.

LUISA: (*rising, offering the pen.*) Sign it, Madam.

MARIE CAROLINE: What's the need? Vanni knows not to suspect where this advice comes from.

LUISA: He could be deceived.

MARIE CAROLINE: What an idea. Fold that letter and give it to me.

LUISA: (*always calm*) May Your Majesty deign to excuse my persistence, but I think it indispensable that your signature be placed at the bottom of this letter.

MARIE CAROLINE: You forget yourself, I think. (*she wants to take the letter, but Luisa crumples it and stepping back a pace burns it at one of the candelabra placed on the left*) Such unparalleled audacity—

LUISA: It's only prudence, madame. I have some enemies and I am protecting myself. This letter, signed by you, is an act of government that I have nothing to do with. Stripped of your signature it could have been a base accusation which I do not intend anyone shall be able to accuse me of.

CARACCIOLO: (*aside*) Heroic child!

LADY HAMILTON: (*with rage*) She's escaping me.

MARIE CAROLINE: (*in a fury*) So that's it! You all hear her? You are making yourself the accomplice of these wretches who are dreaming of ruining the state.

LUISA: I am only the accomplice of my dignity, Madame. I am only fighting for my honor here.

MARIE CAROLINE: And your honor doubtless consists of thwarting the course of my justice, by protecting those it condemns.

LUISA: I don't want anyone to make them believe through perfidy that it is I who betrayed them.

MARIE CAROLINE: To cling to this degree to the esteem of traitors conspiring against our person. That's to associate oneself in their conspiracies.

LUISA: I never thought, Madame, that self respect could become a crime of state.

MARIE CAROLINE: Take care I don't order Vanni to apprehend you tomorrow.

LUISA: If you hope that he will, at the same time, show me the way to treason, I can assure you that he will waste his effort.

MARIE CAROLINE: That's too much. Let the Chevaliere San Felice be escorted to her apartments. We will decide her fate tonight.

CARACCIOLO: (*to Luisa, in a loud voice*) Your hand, noble child. Remember that whatever happens, Prince Francois Caracciolo is honored to call himself your friend, and that you will find him always ready to be your witness whatever the accusation you may be charged with. (*Luisa goes toward the back*)

MARIE CAROLINE: Admiral. Now there's a challenge that will cost you dear.

CARACCIOLO: I render homage to the courageous probity and honor of that dear child, madame. Is that a challenge to someone? I was unaware of it.

LUISA: Thanks, prince. (*she leaves*)

MARIE CAROLINE: (*in prey to a sort of frenetic rage*) Has it come to the point that they think they can outrage me to my face? If the Jacobins of Naples have accomplices and spies in the palace of the Queen of Two Sicilies, let them learn from my mouth she will never succumb through weakness like my sister, Marie Antoinette in France. Yes, I declare to you, if it's necessary to decimate the kingdom, to deliver to Vanni the 20,000 heads he demands, I swear it, I will choke this spirit of revolt and impiety. I will reason with this execrable revolution. Acton, you will inform Vanni that he no longer need be embarrassed by the pretended privileges of this insolent noble woman. Any noble who betrays is degraded by his crime. (*casting a glance at Caracciolo*) And were he a prince, I would concede him a fresh rope. That's all he can expect from our justice. They think we are already defeated and in our death throws and reduced to mercy. Thanks to God and General Mack victory crowns our efforts. We will no longer see standing before us the specter of this cursed France. (*the crack of a coachman's whip can be heard in the distance.*) And wait. Wait. That's the courier that the King announced to us who's arriving. Championnet has been exterminated. We've triumphed. (*The door opens violently. The King appears followed by D'Ascoli. With a shout of stupefaction*) The King!

(*The King rushes in covered with dust, boots muddy, hair unpowdered. He is dressed very simply. D'Ascoli, on the contrary is dressed in the King's clothes with all his decorations.*)

KING: (*after having strode around and looked at everyone present without speaking to them*) Brrr! It's better here than on the road from Albano. What do you say to it, D'Ascoli? By the way, we are hungry, very hungry. The rest of you have eaten. As for us, since leaving Rome we haven't had a morsel to put between our teeth. Ah, indeed! Quick! A chicken, a pate, whatever you've got. In two place settings. I have a raging hunger.

MARIE CAROLINE: Serve the King. (*they bring a platter to the table on the right*)

KING: Yuck! What bad inns there are in my kingdom. And how I pity the poor devils who count on them. Come to table, D'Ascoli. (*they sit*)

MARIE CAROLINE: Sire—

KING: (*attacking his chicken*) What, madame?

MARIE CAROLINE: Our unease is extreme. To what circumstance do we owe this unhoped for and sudden return?

KING: (*a slice of quail in his fist*) Madame, you told me, I think, the history of Francis the First, who was, after I don't know what battle, the prisoner of I don't know which Emperor—writing to his mother a long letter which ended with a pretty phrase "all is lost save honor."

MARIE CAROLINE: (*becoming pale*) What's the connection.

KING: Well, suppose I am arriving from Pavia. That's the name of the battle, I recall now. Suppose then, I am arriving from Pavia, and not having been stupid enough to let myself be captured like King Francis the First, instead of writing you, I've come to tell you myself.

MARIE CAROLINE: (*weakly*) All is lost, save honor!

KING: (*with a strident laugh*) Oh, no, Madame. There's a slight variation. All is lost. Even honor!

D'ASCOLI: (*protesting*) Sire. You are exaggerating.

KING: If honor wasn't lost, D'Ascoli, after the way those folks ran. I paid a ducat and a half for guides and I still had all the trouble in the world to pass by them? After the shame. (*General silence. The King uncorks a bottle, tosses the cork in the air, then fills his glass and raises it in a toast.*) To the health of Championnet! Now there's a man of his word. He promised the Republicans to be in Rome before the twentieth day and he is there on the seventeenth.

MARIE CAROLINE: What, Sir? Championnet is in Rome?

KING: As surely as I am in Caserta.

MARIE CAROLINE: What! General Mack who was so strong with his 60,000 men. Crushed by the 10,000 Republicans of Championnet?

KING: Your Mack is an imbecile. He ought to run himself through and ride post haste. And if we heard the cannon all day it was our own artillery used by the French, who, lacking their own, used ours to destroy my own soldiers.

MARIE CAROLINE: (*allowing herself to fall into an armchair near Lady Hamilton*) Why, this is a disaster.

KING: I strongly invite you not to doubt it. I might have left my skin there but for D'Ascoli.

MARIE CAROLINE: What—this masquerade?

KING: Yes. D'Ascoli dressed as the King. Me, dressed as the Duke D'Ascoli. Tell them about it, Duke, tell them—

D'ASCOLI: It's not for me to boast of the honors that Your Majesty did me.

KING: He calls that an honor! Poor D'Ascoli. Well, as for me, I am going to tell you. About the honor I did him. It appears these wretched Jacobins have said they would hang me if I fell into their hands.

MARIE CAROLINE: And they would really have been capable of it.

KING: That's exactly what I thought. Then at Albano, I said to D'Ascoli. Give me your clothes, take mine; if these tatterdemalion Jacobins should catch us, they will think you are the King and let me scamper off. You will explain to them later, when I am well away, very well away, that they are mistaken and they will release you. Only (*laughing loudly*) D'Ascoli didn't think of one thing. It's that if we'd been taken, they wouldn't have given him time to explain and would have begun by hanging him.

D'ASCOLI: (*very simply*) I beg Your Majesty's pardon. I did think of it and that's why I accepted.

KING: (*touched, rising*) You thought of it and you accepted?

D'ASCOLI: Yes, Sire.

KING: Well, my friend, then you're a better man than I am. And that's a thing I won't forget in my life. You will keep these clothes, D'Ascoli. You will keep them with its sashes and its medals in memory of the day you offered to save the life of your King. And D'Ascoli, if ever you have a favor to ask me, or a reproach to make me, you will put on this uniform and you will come to me.

CARACCIOLO: Fine, Sire! Now that's the way to talk.

KING: Ah, it's you, Admiral. Now here we are in a bad pass, my old sea wolf. And if I'd followed your advice and that of Ruffo all this would never have happened.

CARACCIOLO: (*looking at Nelson*) It's just that the Cardinal and I, Sire, are real Neapolitans and that we want the best for the state.

NELSON: (*aside*) The insolent.

KING: (*rising and tossing away his napkin*) Finally. We must make a decision. (*As the danger of the situation sinks in on the courtiers they gradually leave so that as Ruffo enters no one remains around the King and Queen except Caracciolo, Ruffo, Acton, Nelson, Andre Backer, Lady Hamilton and D'Ascoli.*)

RUFFO: Yes, sire. And just in time. Naples is awaiting you, sire. Your place is at Naples.

MARIE CAROLINE: (*leaping from her seat*) In Naples, Cardinal? Is Your Eminence in league with our enemies?

RUFFO: Me, Madam?

MARIE CAROLINE: To advise the King to return to Naples! Is that a loyal servant? The court must move to Palermo. Only there, under the protection of the brave Nelson, will I feel myself sheltered from all peril.

KING: Hey! Hey! The fact is that in Sicily—

RUFFO: Sire, do you want the people of Naples to feel you are abandoning them? The army is broken, but you can rally it.

KING: And who will undertake that?

CARACCIOLO: I, sire! I have under my orders 4,000 proven marines. I will answer to defend the routes with them. I will fortify them. When your soldiers see how the marines die, they will rally behind them.

MARIE CAROLINE: Fine promises. You could be killed, Admiral. And the ways will be forced.

CARACCIOLO: There will be time then to embark, Madame. You have in port three fleets. Yours, the Portuguese Flotilla, and the Fleet of His Britannic Majesty.

KING: After all, Madame, he's right. No rush.

MARIE CAROLINE: Tomorrow all the roads will be in the hands of the French.

RUFFO: We will oppose a nation to them.

MARIE CAROLINE: How?

RUFFO: Neapolitans fight badly in flat country. But our mountaineers are terrible in their home area. Let the Admiral hold them off only eight days, and, as for me, I will answer for the rest.

KING: You, Cardinal?

RUFFO: Fifty towns and 200 villages will rise to defend the Neapolitan soil. For this I have only to proclaim a Holy War. The French can come then. I will stir up a fire against them which will consume them.

KING: Why, that's a superb revenge.

MARIE CAROLINE: What has produced this Roman fanaticism? Are they armed only to defend Saint Peter?

KING: Hum! And you, Milord Nelson; do you have advice to give us?

NELSON: Sire, I comprehend the illusions of Admiral Caracciolo and His Eminence, the Cardinal. But I don't share them.

KING: Ah!

CARACCIOLO: Sire, I beg you not to listen to foreign advice which puts your throne in jeopardy. Milord Nelson cannot be taken for a judge in matters demanding Neapolitan honor.

NELSON: Perhaps, Admiral. But I can be a good judge of Neapolitan cowardice.

CARACCIOLO: (*putting his hand on his sword*) Milord. (*The King subdues him with a gesture*)

NELSON: (*persisting*) Sire, you can no longer confide yourself to men who have abandoned you, be it through cowardice or through treachery.

CARACCIOLO: Every people has its hours of defeat, sire. These French, before whom we are fleeing, had their Civita-Castellana three times. Poitiers, Crécy, Agincourt. But a single victory sufficed to erase these defeats: Fontenoy!

KING: (*low to Caracciolo*) Fontenoy. Ah! Ah! Nicely alluded to, my Admiral.

MARIE CAROLINE: Sire, leave then for Naples, where perhaps tomorrow, the Jacobins will be masters. Deliver your life to them, that of our children, mine. But take care that one day or the next you don't find yourself on the square of the palace—on the scaffold like Louis XVI.

KING: (*starting*) The scaffold! Hey! Madame! I have no more taste for that than you yourself. The scaffold. They would dare. Yeah! The French would indeed hang me. What we are going to do is not very valiant or very brave. But, still. You wish it. We will go to Sicily.

MARIE CAROLINE: (*with joy*) At last!

KING: I am angry about it, Ruffo. Your plan suits me. Your plan, too, Admiral. But what! As for me, I've never been brave. The struggle—that's not my affair. And then the scaffold. What the devil?

MARIE CAROLINE: Everything is prepared, Sire. Through prudence our precautions were taken.

KING: Touching confidence in our success.

MARIE CAROLINE: The carriages are waiting, harnessed in the stables, and in three quarters of an hour we can reach the beach.

NELSON: You can embark, sire.

KING: That's fine. Come on, then. But we won't be the first to hightail it— Look everywhere is empty around us. Ah, D'Ascoli. All I see in this stampede makes me better understand what you are worth. (*He leaves with D'Ascoli. Nelson, Acton, Backer. The Queen and Lady Hamilton leave by the right. Ruffo and Caracciolo look at each other with indignation.*)

RUFFO: They are leaving without looking behind them. Abandoning their kingdom to anarchy. Delivering our towns to the foreigner. Well, what they dare not do for the honor of my country, for the defense of the throne, and the altar, I will attempt, myself. Alone.

CARACCIOLO: Listen. In the distance. You'd say it was the crackling of gunfire.

RUFFO: Why, look there. Heaven is on fire by the side of Naples. (*on the terrace, fire can be seen on the horizon.*)

NANNO: (*appearing on the terrace arms extended to the horizon*) Those are the goodbyes of Lord Nelson, Caracciolo. It's the Neapolitan fleet, burning.

CARACCIOLO: Infamy! My ships burning!

RUFFO: Why, it's like delirium.

CARACCIOLO: (*raising his head*) Come, general without a command, admiral without a fleet. You army alone remains to you and now you have the right to offer it to your country. I am returning to Naples.

RUFFO: And as for me, I am returning to Calabria. Regardless of the King.

CARACCIOLO: The Nation above all!

CURTAIN

ACT IV

SCENE 5

A square in Naples with a view of the street of Toledo. To the right, a house with a balcony in the Spanish style; Luisa's dwelling. To the left the apse of a church whose flying buttresses of stone serve to hide sharpshooters. The interior of the church must be visible through the door in the apse, with the priest on the steps of the altar. To the left, closer to the audience, a cabaret café. The windows and balconies of the houses must all be usable. Barricades formed by thick planks and casks at several points. Michele has a rifle in his hand. In the distance, intermittent firing, and the sound of the tocsin. Lazzaroni in arms enter in groups and call each other. Michele stops before the house on the right to reload. Angiolina opens the door.

ANGIOLINA: So you are continuing to fight?

MICHELE: What do you want? The powder intoxicates. Ah, I don't hold much for shooting at the French who are the comrades of Mr. Salvato. But what! The comrades insisted. Once involved you want to do like the others and even better.

ANGIOLINA: (*noticing a kerchief around his face*) You are wounded?

MICHELE: A scratch, a ricochet. (*pulling up the kerchief*) See. It's not bleeding any more. (*increased firing*) You'd say the assault is going to begin again.

ANGIOLINA: The battle has lasted without relief for five days and five nights.

MICHELE: Yes, and the French have carried our streets house by house, after having seized the gates of the city, its ramparts and its forts. Today they are in the heart of Naples. All resistance is concentrated in this quarter where we are still hanging on. Ah, they are tough soldiers and if I weren't a Neapolitan, I'd be French.

ANGIOLINA: (*taking his hand covered with black powder*) Well, if they must seize it, return home and wash your hands then let this be over.

MICHELE: Heaven. The forts are bombarding us! They haven't for a long time. (*kissing her*) Goodbye, Lina. A ball is quickly taken and if I don't see you again—

ANGIOLINA: How stupid you are! There is no danger.

MICHELE: Huh!

ANGIOLINA: I am quite sure you will see me again.

MICHELE: Bah!

ANGIOLINA: (*an arm around his neck*) Since you must die by hanging! (*she goes with him to the barricade while San Felice and Caracciolo leave the house.*)

SAN FELICE: My word, my dear Prince, if the battle doesn't put an end to the struggle, I fear indeed that the French bombs from the Chateau Neuf will drive us from the asylum you've graciously offered Luisa and me in your palace.

CARACCIOLO: In that case, we will leave by the port and we can await events in Capri. But I wanted to be present at the entry of Championnet.

SAN FELICE: The Junta is holding itself in permanent sittings.

CARACCIOLO: Yes. They've received news from Cardinal Ruffo. They say he's marching on Naples with his army of fanatics.

SAN FELICE: The French will be masters of the city before the Cardinal can give a strong supporting hand to this pack of maddened lazzaroni.

CARACCIOLO: Yes. But afterwards? (*they leave. Pasquale di Simone and Beccaio appear in the door of the café and observe the departure of San Felice and the Admiral.*)

PASQUALE: (*pointing to the house on the right*) It's indeed there that this San Felice is lodging now. If it was only a question of disposing of her. For the last week, with all this tumult we could easily have put a bullet in her heart.

BECCAIO: Yes. But the English woman wants her alive.

PASQUALE: And a thousand ducats are the reward.

BECCAIO: Patience. I've sworn to give her the joy of this revenge. And the opportunity will present itself. (*they leave. The firing has greatly increased in the street. Masked Lazzaroni are in the recesses of the church or behind the shutters of houses. They fire, as do the defenders of the barricades, kneeling behind their barrels. Suddenly a stampede. Men commanded by Friar Pacifico are giving ground. He arrives, furious, running after them, his soutane hitched up, a musket in hand, a stick in the other. He rallies them and roughs them up.*)

FRA PACIFICO: Come on, loafers, stragglers, rabbit hearts. Do you think I am going to let you give ground? Dogs of poltroons. Neapolitans of clay. For a nasty grenade bursting between your legs.

BAMBINO: Eh! By the Madonna, we are betrayed. It's the fort of Saint Elmo firing on us.

SECOND LAZZARONI: The Jacobins of Naples are allied with the French.

PACIFICO: (*roughing them up*) Gallows birds, cowards. To the firing, to the firing! And be quick about it.

BAMBINO: Eh! Eh! Is it Saint Francis who will patch us up, if they hurt us?

FIRST LAZZARONI: Look. The Tricolor flag is floating over Chateau Neuf.

PACIFICO: (*to Michele*) Come, Michele. Give an example to these ragged dancing jacks who've got only turnip juice in their veins.

MICHELE: Ah, by Jove. I've been giving them an example for the last five days.

BAMBINO: This is enough work for nothing. As for me, I'm going to take my siesta.

PACIFICO: Remember, my son, that Naples has in its arms a mace that bites and kicks.

BAMBINO: Eh! Soon we won't have any more cartridges to bite. What do you want us to gnaw on?

PACIFICO: You deserve a donkey for an emblem. The most cowardly of quadrupeds. (*increasing shooting off.*)

MICHELE: It's heating up! Forward! By Saint Janvier if we let them cross the square of Vieux Marche the city is taken.

ALL: Attack the French!

FRA PACIFICO: Death to the impious! Death to the Jacobins! (*the battle resumes more furiously. Cannon and rifle fire. Soon the French drums are heard beating the charge, and behind the barricade the republicans arrive, bayonets in the lead, with sappers armed with axes and clubs to break down the barricades. The Lazzaroni of Michele and Pacifico attempt to struggle hand to hand but a squadron of cavalry led by Salvato sabers them and forces them to disperse.*)

BAMBINO: (*escaping*) Pacifico, my old friend, watch your fleas!

PACIFICO: (*casting away his baton and musket*) The Devil is with them. It's a question of making a good retreat back to the convent. (*seeing a second squad of Frenchmen he tosses Bambino to the ground*) Close your eyes and play dead. (*kneeling by him and murmuring prayers over him, telling his beads.*)

REGULUS: Eh! Say, Capuchin. You were shooting at us just now from behind your barricade.

PACIFICO: Me? Holy Mother of God who has never harmed so much as a chicken! I have a rosary for my weapon.

REGULUS: Your rosary resembles this here musket rather much. It's still quite hot.

PACIFICO: I pray for the dead. I give absolution for the dying.

SOLDIER: You stink of gunpowder. (*plunging his hands into his pockets.*) And you still have pockets full of cartridges.

PACIFICO: Help, Good Christians! They are violating a servant of God. (*runs off pursued by some soldiers. Bambino crawls the length of the wall and slips off to the left. General Championnet arrives accompanied by his staff officers and Nicolino and stops before the Café on the left.*)

NICOLINO: General, Naples is yours now. But if you want our bourgeoisie, terrorized by the lazzaroni, to greet you with joy, you must reassure them by examples. Things would have been over five days ago but for these gangs of pillagers who refused to release their prey.

REGULUS: (*leading in Michele*) General, here's a fanatic who was defending the last barricade all by himself.

CHAMPIONNET: I said it. Shoot this character for me.

MICHELE: (*to himself*) Decidedly, Nanno was mistaken. I am not a colonel; and I am not going to be hanged.

ANGIOLINA: (*appearing on the balcony at the right*) Oh, my God! Why, it's Michele, my poor Michele, they've got there.

MICHELE: (*pushing away the bandage offered him*) The General said to shoot me, but he didn't say to cover my eyes. (*noticing Salvato who has just arrived to join Championnet*) Blood of Christ, Mr. Salvato, tell them I am quite capable of dying without having my eyes covered.

SALVATO: Michele! General, this brave lad saved my life. You won't refuse me mercy for him. (*he hugs Michele and leads him before Championnet. Little by little the bourgeois are leaving their houses. The women and the people come to look at the soldiers and the General.*)

CHAMPIONNET: (*after a conversation with Salvato and Nicolino*) Neapolitans. However, severe you will find me towards rebellion, you will find me as just for services rendered. (*to Michele*) You saved the life of one of my officers. Not only do I grant you mercy, but I want to reward you. What rank did you have among your companions?

MICHELE: I was Captain, Excellency. But it seems I must not stop there. It's foretold that I will be a Colonel and then hanged.

CHAMPIONNET: (*smiling*) All I can do, and all I want to do, is charge myself with the first part of the prediction. I am going to make you a Colonel in the Service of the Parthenopean Republic. Organize your regiment. I will furnish you the pay and I will make you the gift of a uniform.

MICHELE: Colonel. I'm a Colonel. Long live General Championnet!

THE BOURGEOIS: Long live General Championnet!

MICHELE: Long live the French! Long live the Parthenopean Republic!

ALL: Long live the Parthenopean Republic!

LUISA: (*to Salvato*) Thanks to heaven here you are safe. I wasn't living. These last five days without news were an agony. Surrounded by a circle of fire, knowing you were at the breach and how little you spare yourself! But at last, here I am delivered of my anguish and very proud of this liberty that Naples is going to owe you.

MICHELE: (*to Angiolina*) Well. Here I am Colonel, Lina!

ANGIOLONA: (*offering her cheek*) Kiss me to celebrate your rank. Why, I will be the Colonel's lady.

MICHELE: Surely. Only we'd really better hasten the wedding for if Nanno really predicted correctly, General Championnet, without intending to just sent me on a giant step towards the rope. (*The General has set up a table in front of the Café and sits writing orders distributed by aides de camp.*)

DOYEN of the CHAPTER of SAINT JANVIER: General, you knew at Rome to forbid the pillaging of the treasures of the basilicas. Do mercy for Saint Janvier as you have done for Saint Peter. You alone at this time can re-establish order in this city given over to anarchy and prevent the scattering of relics and the ruin of our Cathedral.

CHAMPIONNET: Signor Doyen. I will stop the pillaging. Calm and tranquility, I promise you, will be reborn in this unfortunate, betrayed, and deceived city. I will even give Saint Janvier a permanent guard who will shelter you against all attempts. But in return, I beg you, what will Saint Janvier do for me.

DOYEN: General, I don't understand—

CHAMPIONNET: I will explain. Saint Janvier, for whom I have a particular veneration has always been a guide to the people of Naples in the great crises of its political life.

DOYEN: But—

CHAMPIONNET: It's necessary today that he be consulted following accustomed usages. Return to the Cathedral. Explore the precious blood on the altar. I know a prayer that Saint Janvier won't remain deaf to. I am therefore certain that ten minutes after the exposure of the precious blood a miracle will occur.

DOYEN: I will observe to you, General, that miracles are produced only in determined periods and that it doesn't depend on the chapter—

CHAMPIONNET: Do you think so, Signor Doyen? (*rapidly writing a few lines*) Nicolino.

NICOLINO: General?

CHAMPIONNET: This is good for 10,000 francs on the army treasury. Payable at sight by the treasurer. (*pointing to the door*) You are going to accompany the doyen and his chapter. If the miracle occurs as I already have reason to believe and said so just now—you will deliver this note to the Doyen. It's an offering by France to Saint Janvier.

DOYEN: General. This generosity. I would like to promise you in return. And yet—

CHAMPIONNET: Wait. (*to Nicolino*) If by a misunderstanding that I don't want to anticipate, Saint Janvier should not hear our prayers—

NICOLINO: What must be done, general?

CHAMPIONNET: (*coldly*) You will place the chapter in its entirety under arrest.

NICOLINO: That's understood!

DOYEN: (*shocked*) Mercy, General.

CHAMPIONNET: You have ten minutes, father.

NICOLINO: (*pulling out his watch*) Ten minutes. (*The Doyen and the bewildered canons reenter the sacristy followed by Nicolino.*)

SALVATO: (*presenting the deputation*) General. The Deputies of the Republican Junta of Naples.

CHAMPIONNET: You are welcome, citizens.

CYRILLO: The notables of the city have charged us with organizing the new powers, and our first care, General, is to come to see you. To put ourselves under your shield, to demand your support. Without you, without your advice, all our efforts would be powerless in the work of reconstruction that we're are going to undertake,

CHAMPIONNET: I know all of you, citizens, through your past struggles and sacrifices. Through your devotion to the national cause. And you can count on me. (*looking at his watch, aside*) Three minutes. (*aloud*) Besides my support you ask my advice. I am going to give you my politics in a few words. Don't preach to the converted. (*aside*) Five minutes. (*aloud*) The Neapolitan populace is a child incapable of comprehending the political philosophy you are familiar with. You are men of science and scholarship. Speak its language, put yourselves in the position of its ignorance, of its fanaticism, make use even of its vices. And don't imagine that it will suffice for you to motivate the reform of morals that are the product of several centuries of corruption by means of an eloquent decree. (*aside*) Eight minutes. (*aloud*) Don't stop a stream, divert it. Don't annul a power, direct it. And when you cannot destroy a superstition by a single blow—profit by it. (*aside*) Ten minutes. (*At this moment the Doyen inside the church can be seen at the altar raising in his arms the bubbling blood of Saint Janvier.*)

VOICES: A miracle has taken place. Long live Saint Janvier. Long live the French.

CHAMPIONNET: Citizens, what you hear is an example of following the precept. Saint Janvier is with us. Here we are masters of Naples for a few days.

MICHELE (*rushing in*) Saint Janvier has spoken. Saint Janvier is for the Republic—Long live the Parthenopean Republic!

THE LAZZARONI: Long Live the Republic! Long Live Saint Janvier. (*Bells ring everywhere. The windows of the houses are paved with French colors and colors of the Neapolitan Republic—yellow, red and blue. A roll of drums. The French Army marches in review past Championnet who stands in front of Luisa's house.*)

VOICES SHOUTING: Long live the Republic! (*After the Army passes by Fragola offers Championnet a magnificent bouquet of flowers in the Neapolitan colors. An improvised orchestra plays and the most beautiful girls of Naples sing the national anthem of Monti.*)

CURTAIN

ACT IV

SCENE 6

The Palace D'Angri. A room occupied by General Salvato Palmieri commander of the Republican Army of Naples. A double door to the left, giving on a room for staff officers. To the right a large window with a view of Naples. Also, on the right a secret door leading to the apartments of the palace. In the back a map of Italy stretched over a Louis XV couch. Chimney to the left. A table with papers, maps spread out, weapons, illuminated lamps. Michele is in the uniform of a Colonel of Volunteers. At rise, Michele sounds the wall with his saber listening to the resonation. But he doesn't find the door. Salvato enters from the left in formal General's uniform, papers in hand. He stops, astonished by what Michele is doing.

SALVATO: Well? What are you doing there, Michele?

MICHELE: Pardon, general, but this devilish palace D'Angri is a box full of surprises. I keep discovering secret corridors and hidden stairways. That doesn't astonish me. The palace D'Angri belonged to the favorite.

SALVATO: Ah. The Lyonna lived here.

MICHELE: For a long while. And all these hiding places, these doges served in her intrigues.

SALVATO: What does that matter?

MICHELE: General, you've done too much good not to have collected a lot of enemies. Since the Directory, may God damn them, has recalled brave General Championnet, it's you who are governing Naples and keeping the pillagers in check. And I know more than one who would willingly plant his dagger in your heart. You see, you have to be careful.

SALVATO: Fine, my dear Michele, the Partisans trouble your brain and you see conspiracies everywhere.

MICHELE: Anyway, let me sound the panels. I have my idea.

SALVATO: Later. Right now I have to entrust you with an urgent mission.

MICHELE: Command, general.

SALVATO: Cardinal Ruffo is already master of the heights. The fort of Carmine is threatened. We must detach it. This is the key to Naples. Here's an order for Schiapino. When night falls let him suppress Ruffo's posts on the ridge tops with his Montagnards, and hold them. Monthonnet will support him by an attack on Ruffo's headquarters in the Madeleine.

MICHELE: Understood, General. In less than a quarter of an hour Schiapino will have the order. (*he leaves*)

SALVATO: (*alone*) The circle is closing around us. And soon the Cardinal's army will have cut off all retreat. Only one exit is possible at this time. To force open the route to Capua. In that direction the French garrison offers us its hand. And we can shelter all the compromised patriots and so many precious lives from the vengeance of the court. The present escapes us. It's the future we must learn to prepare. But does the Grand Council understand it? (*Caracciolo appears. Salvato rushes to him*) Well?

CARACCIOLO: They didn't understand. For the hundredth time it is prejudice and grandiose phrases that move them. For the last two months we've let them legislate at their ease, accepting for ourselves alone, the entire responsibility for the struggle. Naples half strangled by the partisans, the internal reaction which raises its head, the lazzaroni who have continued with great care to sharpen their knives for revenge. All this seems not to exist for them. They are keeping themselves busy by decreeing the application of the decimal system in all the Neapolitan provinces without realizing that the empire of their laws ends at the extremity of the rue Toledo.

SALVATO: So the incessant progress of Ruffo, the daily decimation of our heroic battalions, the reduction of our forces to a few thousand men doesn't open their eyes to the approaching catastrophe?

CARACCIOLO: No. The news of a French fleet leaving Toulon makes them hope that the Directory, reversing its decisions intends to again intervene in their favor. And this chimera intoxicates them.

SALVATO: I wanted to save Naples—since they refuse, there's nothing to do but to pay Ruffo dearly for the agony of our liberties. (*An aide-de-camp introduces the Chevalier, Luisa and Angiolina.*)

SALVATO: You, Chevalier, and you, madame.

SAN FELICE: My dear General. The bombardment is depriving us of our last asylum. My house at Infrascata is in flames. I don't see any place but the palace of D'Angri where Luisa can be safe. I am bringing her to you. I know your heart, Salvato. It's my daughter, my beloved child that I confide to you. And I know what ever happens you will defend her as a cherished sister.

SALVATO: In the supreme crisis we are going through, Chevalier, you couldn't bring me a greater joy. My life answers for hers.

SAN FELICE: While you improvise a place for her to stay, as for me I am returning to Monthonnet.

LUISA: Already?

SAN FELICE: It's necessary. Night never passes without an alarm.

LUISA: (*to Salvato*) Come General, show us the way. Follow us, Angiolina. (*they leave.*)

SAN FELICE: Poor children. I am the obstacle.

CARACCIOLO: What are you saying?

SAN FELICE: They love each other. Don't you know it? How could it have been otherwise? By placing them face to face one day, both young, both beautiful and sensitive. Fate decreed it.

CARACCIOLO: What! You think?

SAN FELICE: My dear Prince, I've seen their love born and grow; I've followed its anguish and its struggles. I know that they can look at me without blushing, for their virtue has not weakened. They are both noble hearts and they can be trusted. You see I don't hesitate.

CARACCIOLO: Yes, you're right. Salvato's soul is capable of the greatest sacrifices.

SAN FELICE: And his courage is capable of the greatest heroism.

CARACCIOLO: If it had been possible to save Naples he would have done it.

SAN FELICE: But I don't want him to dream of engulfing himself in the great shipwreck of the nation. He was conquered by fate. He must live. By confiding the care of Luisa to him I am saving him from despair. And as for me, at this point, I can dispose of my life as a citizen. Something Luisa must no longer be involved in.

CARACCIOLO: My noble friend. Are these farewells you are making me? Isn't it enough to brave death without running ahead of it?

SAN FELICE: Admiral, death alone gives release. Luisa has never been anything but my child. To assure the future of the orphan girl, the crazy idea came to me of giving her my name. Ah, if I could live by reducing myself to the sweet role of father. Goodbye, Prince. If you don't see me again, you will tell her that in falling I blessed the blow that struck me, since it allowed me to bequeath her the right to be happy.

CARACCIOLO: Ah, I can't leave you this way. (*they leave. The room remains empty for a moment. Then one of the panels that Michele did not test slides back revealing a secret corridor. Beccaio enters furtively, his face hideous, knife in hand.*)

BECCAIO: The English woman spoke correctly. Through this secret passage from the alleyway, you arrive here in a second. So, I've got this damned Salvato at the tip of my knife. He can say his paternosters. Someone's coming. (*rushing back in, shutting the panel.*)

MICHELE'S VOICE: (*entering violently with the staff officers*) By Saint Janvier! This time no one will accuse me of daydreaming!

SALVATO: (*coming in*) What's the matter with you, Michele?

MICHELE: General, I've got them.

SALVATO: Eh! Who have you got?

MICHELE: My conspirators.

SALVATO: Again.

MICHELE: Oh, this time I've got my proofs, and even a living one.

SALVATO: Explain yourself.

MICHELE: I was returning from taking the order to Schiapino who by now must have already begun his action, when I noticed suspicious shadows which stopped from one door to the next. Why? I slid along their path. I verified the villains were placing a red cross on the homes of our best patriots. Once determined, I said to myself, I need my witness. I was alone but on horseback. I galloped up, I fell on the crowd. I grabbed one by the collar and dragged him here at a gallop. And if you want to question him.

SALVATO: So be it. Bring him and leave us.

(*Michele brings in the prisoner who has his hat pulled down. Michele leaves. Once Michele is gone the prisoner lets his cloak fall and is revealed as Lady Hamilton disguised as a mountaineer from the Abruzzi. Her hair is messed up falling over her shoulders, her tie undone, her dress torn in the struggle leaves her breast partially uncovered. Salvato, recoils.*) You!

LADY HAMILTON: Yes. In your hands. At your mercy. The roles are reversed. Three months ago at the Villa San Felice I could have destroyed you with a word, delivering you to Vanni. I didn't want to. But what's the difference. You have a beautiful revenge. Profit by it.

SALVATO: (*looking at her coldly and severely; he goes to the table and takes a pen*) By what gate do you want to leave Naples? I am going to sign you a safe conduct.

LADY HAMILTON: (*ironic*) Truly. Such grandeur of soul.

SALVATO: (*seated at the table*) One bit of advice. You are playing a dangerous game. Take care. Not just for myself. I am worried about the red crosses you are drawing on our doors. But you could fall into the hands of an officer less inclined to scorn your plots, to forget your past.

LADY HAMILTON: (*very agitated*) Ah! (*making an effort to remain calm*) I will leave by the gate to Pausilippa.

SALVATO: (*giving her the pass*) Here.

LADY HAMILTON: (*taking the safe conduct and slipping it into her bosom. Then seizing his hand and pressing it against her*) Ah, Salvato, if you had loved me!

SALVATO: (*glacial*) Milady, if I had loved you, I would not have at this time the power to get you out of a very bad situation. (*pushing her away*) Because my despair and your shame would have killed me a long while ago.

LADY HAMILTON: Pitiless heart! What have I done to you to make you treat me like this? I adored you with a mad passion; that's my crime. For you, to follow you, to belong to you, I would have given up everything, sacrificed everything. You know that quite well. What do you call my shame? Did I choose the conditions into which I was born? Until I was fifteen wealth for me was whatever could satisfy my hunger. Evil was what attracted insults and beatings to me. It was when my heart beat for the first time that I understood what you wanted to say with your great word virtue. And it's for you, for you alone that I regretted my past. Oh, then I wept tears of rage. But all my efforts to redeem myself, to atone, you've paid only with scorn.

SALVATO: If you've suffered such anguish I pity you.

LADY HAMILTON: Pity! Yes, that's all I'm worth, right? Love is for the immaculate who have no need to struggle or conquer. But my pride revolts. It's my virtue, and it's my strength. In London, I made all the Puritans of Parliament grovel at my feet. At Naples you know just how far I've been able to climb. More than Queen Caroline I dispose of the fortune of the state. How do you know if tomorrow I won't command here in my turn? Well! Salvato, my hopes of revenge, the joys of power, the intoxications of pride—all those things Cardinal Ruffo and his Calabrians are working at this very moment to deliver to me. And I will give it all for one smile from your mouth. All for one look of tenderness. For one word of forgiveness escaping from your lips.

SALVATO: Ah! Shut up!

LADY HAMILTON: Why do you condemn my heart to hate? Ah, if you knew how it cares for you with ineffable sweetness, submission, devotion, passionate adoration, you wouldn't have the strength to repulse me.

SALVATO: Enough! Enough blasphemies, wretch! Are you forgetting who you are, who I am? Where we are? You dare to speak to me of love, of tenderness. You ask for pardon. Pardon! (*suddenly he opens the window revealing Naples*) Why, look there. We are in Naples.

And Naples is my country. We are in Naples where you personify the genius of evil. Naples ruined by you. Naples betrayed by you. Delivered, decimated by you. And which you promise to butcher again tomorrow.

LADY HAMILTON: (*recoiling*) God!

SALVATO: Why I need only lean out this window to cry your name in the square in the silence of the night. To that detested name a nation would rise up in horror. A hundred thousand voices would demand justice. A hundred thousand shouts for death would rise up to you.

LADY HAMILTON: (*terror stricken*) Ah, silence, mercy. Silence. You speak the truth. They hate me. Yes, the whole world hates me. Oh, but just wish it, I can make it all good. Command, and I'll stop the struggle. Say one word and the nation will owe me its liberty.

SALVATO: (*with scorn*) What dream are you dreaming? Why your hands are red with the blood of these Neapolitans that you wish to dishonor with your charity.

LADY HAMILTON: (*with rage*) What! I humiliate myself. I abase myself. I beg. And I receive only outrages and scorn. It's your Luisa who separates us. It's that San Felice woman who shuts me out of your heart.

SALVATO: (*instinctively moving to place himself protectively before the door that Luisa went through*) Luisa!

LADY HAMILTON: (*guessing correctly*) She's here. With you. Ah! Ah! Ah! The virtuous spouse!

SALVATO: (*impatient, in a rage*) Shut up!

LADY HAMILTON: There they are! These honest women; who understand so well how to adjust their modesty to the voluptuous pleasures of adultery.

SALVATO: (*driving her away with a gesture*) Leave!

LADY HAMILTON: Yes, Salvato, I'm leaving. But I am taking my revenge with me. You reproach me for my past. Tomorrow her shame will pay me for your scorn. (*she takes a step to leave*)

SALVATO: (*terrible, barring her way*) Wretch! This is too much. My generosity wears out at last. The justice of Naples demands you. Henceforth you belong to it. Let you cross this doorway? No! I would be responsible for your crimes before God. You shan't leave. Rather, viper, I will crush you in my claws.

LUISA: (*appearing to the left*) Salvato!

LADY HAMILTON: (*with rage*) Her!

SALVATO: Luisa!

LUISA: Let that door free, my friend. Let this woman leave. Her insults will fall back on her. Her slanders cannot reach me. How little this unfortunate woman understands the chaste and holy friendship that unites us! The pure joys of sacrifice are not accessible except to exalted souls! Go! Her hate is powerless. For victorious duty makes our consciences strong. And no one will know how to prevent both of us from proceeding in life with firm hearts and heads high.

SALVATO: (*hesitating*) Be merciful to her. You wish it?

LUISA: Yes.

SALVATO: (*making way for Lady Hamilton*) Go on! But remember.

LADY HAMILTON: (*in a cold rage*) Yes. I will remember. (*picking up her mantle and hurling a menacing glance at them*) Watch over her carefully, your Luisa! (*she leaves hurriedly*)

(*Salvato takes a step in pursuit but Luisa stops him with a gesture.*)

SALVATO: (*with a gesture of disgust*) The infamous creature. She's threatening again. Ah, Luisa! I am afraid your pity has made me commit a mistake.

LUISA: No, my Salvato. A soldier such as you doesn't give up a woman whatever her crimes may be. (*thunder of cannon in the distance*)

SALVATO: That's not the cannon of Schiapino. What are those lights flashing on the heights? (*distant murmur of voices can be heard*) And in the rue Toledo. Those voices, those torches. (*they move toward the balcony.*)

LUISA: Another riot?

HECTOR: (*entering, followed by Nicolino and Michele*) My dear General, I think the night will be serious. They are testing us on all sides. Fra Diavolo, Mammone, Pronio, all Cardinal Ruffo's lieutenants seem to be attacking at the same time. (*at the entry of the officers, Luisa retires to the balcony and conceals herself.*)

MICHELE: And Fra Pacifico is running through the town stirring up the lazzaroni. Declaring Saint Janvier fallen as the patron of Naples.

SALVATO: They want to set those cursed dogs on our heels while we are defending the walls and gates. That's the strategy of the Church. But we will resist them everywhere at once; we will show them that we still have teeth to chew with. (*sits at his table*) This advice to the Admiral. Let him moor his fleet at Portici and protect the approaches with several volleys of grape shot. This order to Monthonnet. He's facing Ruffo, I will bring him reinforcements. You Michele—are your men ready?

MICHELE: Bridals in hand, ready to leap into the saddle to fall upon the lazzaroni.

SALVATO: Sweep the rue Toledo. Occupy the Vieux Marche. Let all the vermin return underground.

MICHELE: Don't worry. My Old Pacifico. You've only tucked up your soutane to run faster. (*he leaves.*)

NICOLINO: And me?

SALVATO: You, Nicolino, must resign yourself not to take part in the struggle unless the cannon in Fort Saint Elmo can no longer be of use to us. The instrument that Championnet gave you in leaving you two French regiments and the command of the fort is formal. Don't deploy your forces or stage a sortie except in an exceptional situation, and on my request. So, tonight I will only ask you to return to your post, to watch our movements, and, if our men are forced to fall back, to support their retreat. With your powerful artillery that's all you can do for us.

NICOLINO: So be it. They appointed me to be opposite Ruffo's headquarters. If he's not out of range I'm going to make a pretty hash of him with Saint Elmo's cannon. (*he leaves. Artillery and rifle fire in the distance.*)

SALVATO: Luisa.

LUISA: (*returning from the balcony*) Duty calls you. Go!

SALVATO: I am going to check the advanced positions and as soon as my measures are taken—

LUISA: Return, Yes, return to bring me a little courage before the battle. I have a presentiment of a misfortune tonight. But if we must succumb, let heaven grant us the joy of dying together.

SALVATO: In an hour I will be near you. (*he leaves.*)

LUISA: I ought to be accustomed to this uproar of cannon. To these noises of battle. For the last two months the struggle has been going on. Tonight, I feel myself all atremble. (*she sits near the table.*) Just now I was looking at my hand. Without thinking about it I saw that cross. (looks at it under the light) It seems to be growing. The track is bloody. (*As Luisa sits absorbed near the table, the moving panel slides back and Beccaio appears followed by Pasquale di Simone and Lady Hamilton, with other bailiffs in the rear. Beccaio slides the door and bolts it; Pasquale with a black sheet in his hand goes behind Luisa and tosses it over her head.*)

Luisa utters a cry stifled by Pasquale who ties her up and carries her off.)

LADY HAMILTON: Go. Get to the port by way of the back alleys. The sloop. Nelson will answer to me for her. (*she leaves followed by Pasquale. Beccaio is about to follow when Angiolina who has arrived in time to see the kidnapping in progress, utters a scream.*)

ANGIOLINA: Help! Help!

BECCAIO: Will you shut up! (*grabs her and knocks her down*)

ANGIOLINA: Ah! Wretch! Michele, Help me!

BECCAIO: Michele. Ah! You'll have it so. (*plunging his knife in her breast. Angiolina falls, screaming. Beccaio escapes behind the panel and shuts it. The door is burst open by Michele and several soldiers*)

MICHELE: (*rushing in*) Angiolina. My soul. My life! Ah. Speak to me.

ANGIOLINA: Ah! You've come too late for me, Michele. Too late for her. They've carried her off.

MICHELE: Carried her off. Who? Luisa.

ANGIOLINA: (*pointing to the panel*) There. The bailiffs. There.

MICHELE: (*to soldiers*) Break down that panel and run. Ah, my Lina. No. You cannot die.

ANGIOLINA: It's over. But you will avenge me.

MICHELE: Ah! I swear it. But his name? Who?

ANGIOLINA: It's—

MICHELE: Well?

ANGIOLINA: Beccaio. (*she dies*)

CURTAIN

ACT V

SCENE 7

A square in Naples on the heights. In the back, a view of Saint Elmo dominating the town, from which the French tricolor flies. A usable ramp which snakes around the back leading to Fort Saint Elmo. The rampart ends at the left of stage on a platform which dominates the lower city. A scaffold with a gallows and blocks has been erected on it. To the right, pillars of a prison. In the rear, houses forming a sort of amphitheatre. Lines of Royal soldiers at the back. Calabrians stand guard around the pillars where Cardinal Ruffo has installed his headquarters. At the door of the prison a group of bailiffs. Also near, the scaffold and the chopping blocks. Crowds of people.

BAMBINO: (*shouting from group to group*) Ask for the proclamation of the State Junta. The report of the special judge on the suspects. Ask for the list of the Jacobins hanged on the Ninth of June?

FRAGOLA: (*to Nanno*) I've been able to get into Fort Saint Elmo.

NANNO: Then he's been warned?

FRAGOLA: Milord Nicolino undertakes to make them leave at nightfall and escort them to Capua in safety.

NANNO: But until then they must find an asylum. The Cardinal is leaving Naples in an hour and can do nothing more for them.

FRAGOLA: I am going to speak to Bambino about it.

ARIOLA: (*coming down the ramp; to D'Ascoli who is crossing the square*) You here. Alone, Duke?

D'ASCOLI: I wanted to see the area the King is going to pass through with my own eyes.

ARIOLA: Oh, don't worry. We are really the masters of Naples.

D'ASCOLI: At what price! They unleashed the lazzaroni on the bourgeoisie. Terror reigns. Everywhere you find gibbets.

BAMBINO: Then there was the execution of the traitor Caracciolo hanged from the great mast of the Minerva by order of Admiral Nelson.

ARIOLA: Poor Admiral. The King still loved him. Why did he permit it?

D'ASCOLI: The King, my dear Count, is very bored in Sicily. It rains there to irritate him, to disrupt his life. It deprives him of all his usual pleasures. Then they depict the Jacobins of Naples as killing his game at Persano or destroying the fish in the reserved waters at Pausilippa. I don't know what else. It makes him furious. His fanatic egoism applauds each new execution. At this hour, Vanni is the man he appreciates most. He's made a Marquis of that carnivorous beast.

ARIOLA: In the past he was moderate, and contained the furors of the cabal.

D'ASCOLI: Today he demands the death penalty and designates the victims with his own hand.

ARIOLA: Yes. He put a price on the head of La San Felice and her husband.

D'ASCOLI: They say the Chevalier died on the ramparts.

ARIOLA: That's the best one could wish for him. Otherwise a gibbet. (*they pass*)

BECCAIO: (*rushes in, looking to see if he is followed. A penitent arrives and crosses the stage without looking at him.*) That huge devil of a penitent seems to attach himself to my path.

PASQUALE: Pretty expedition. We didn't take fifty steps to the port when we fell in with a patrol of Jacobins and to escape we had to release La San Felice. I've had to put all my men in the country in the hope of recapturing her so we can get the reward. No one knows what's become of her. (*the Penitent reappears again.*)

BECCAIO: That penitent again.

PASQUALE: At least we've got the husband.

LA BECCAIO: There.

PASQUALE: With a batch of rebels who will take a short hop from this gate to those gibbets.

BECCAIO: (*uneasy*) I want to see their grimaces. (*they go into the prison. The penitent crosses the stage and places himself in observation behind the scaffold. In the shed by the pillars occupied by the Cardinal's soldiers Nanno puts her hand on the shoulder of a Calabrian whose face is hidden by his hat. The soldier turns his head. It's Salvato, with Luisa.*)

SALVATO: Is it the hour, mother?

NANNO: Not yet. The streets are paved with spies. But when the Cardinal passes—let the troops pass by. As for me, I will make the way free and I will escort you to the retreat I've chosen. Tonight the French at Fort Saint Elmo will receive you. Tomorrow you will be at Capua.

LUISA: Alas, Nanno. What will become of us? Here I am already close to the death you predicted for me! The scaffold is there.

NANNO: Shut up! It required an expiatory victim. And your spouse sacrifices himself.

LUISA: Poor friend! Struck down in the attack on San Martino. And I was unable to receive his last goodbyes. (*distant uproar.*)

LAZZARONI: (*in the distance*) Long Live Nosey! Long Live Ferdinand!

NANNO: It's the King. Take care. (*they disappear under the shed. The Calabrians put themselves in arms and form ranks. The King appears on horseback in hunting outfit accompanied by Ariola and D'Ascoli with his household guards.*)

LAZZARONI: Long live Nosey! Death to the Jacobins! (*arrived at the scaffold, the King stares at Saint Elmo, then dismounts gesturing for D'Ascoli to do likewise.*)

KING: Ah, indeed. My vision is blurred.

ARIOLA: What do you mean, sire?

KING: You have good eyes, D'Ascoli. Take a peek up there. Above the houses. What do you see?

D'ASCOLI: Why, sire, what you yourself must see. The fort of Saint Elmo.

KING: Right. And on the fort. The rag fluttering in the wind. That's not the royal flag as I see it?

D'ASCOLI: Assuredly not, sire. I am forced to agree. It's the tricolor of France.

KING: Which means the French are there. Still there. And holding the fort. Which means if I hadn't put my nose in the air just in time I was stupidly going to offer myself as a target to their cannons.

ARIOLA: But, Sire, the truce—

KING: The truce. The good letter to La Châtre. If I was a Republican and a King was passing within the trajectory of my cannon—that would suffice. So this is what Mr. Acton calls being master of Naples. And Lord Nelson who declares that I have nothing to fear. The Queen asserted this morning that I could go hunting at Persano without uneasiness. Yeah! With Fort Saint Elmo and the French at my back! Never in life!

RUFFO: (*who has remained in his camp until the entry of the King, advancing*) If it had been up to me, Sire, it would have been otherwise.

KING: Ah, it's you, Cardinal. I thought you were already far from Naples.

RUFFO: I am leaving for Potenza, Sire. Following your orders, I am going to send back the soldiers of the faith to their mountains. Since Lord Nelson and his English suffice to assure your security.

KING: Yes, indeed. The Queen explained to me you've sent me your resignation. You've been wounded and I don't know the measures the situation demands. But what the devil! Cardinal, as you knew so well how to reopen the gates of Naples for us, you really must have work to complete to prevent the French from taking us in the flank.

RUFFO: Sire, the capitulation which I signed in virtue of my powers as Vicar General returned all of Naples to you and not only are the French leaving Fort Saint Elmo, they are evacuating Capua to you. Foreigners no longer remain in the kingdom.

KING: Well?

RUFFO: That capitulation was torn up. They pressed on my name an inerasable blot. And the slime spurts back on you. A distracted people misunderstood your power. But at last, it is submitting to your laws. I thought that the interests of the kingdom demanded forgetfulness, pardon—

KING: Forgetfulness, pardon—

RUFFO: But in scorn of a sacred act they tore from their refuge those who relied on my word. Everywhere scaffolds are erected. They are condemned without being heard. They are being struck down without a trial.

KING: Are you mad? Do you expect me to pardon these rogues who made me spend five of the most unpleasant months of my life in Sicily?

RUFFO: Sire, justice which resembles vengeance is bad. Think of the terrible tomorrows which you are preparing by means of a merciless repression.

KING: The Devil! You are taking a bad attitude now. Look at all this ruckus over hanging some Jacobins. Don't I have a right to protect myself? And you want them to be accorded clemency at the first opportunity? Not so stupid! As for me, I don't care about returning to Palermo. And I intend to rid myself of them. Oh, yeah—from first to last. And as fast as possible. By steel, by the rope, by water, anyway you please. But I don't intend to talk with that rabble any further. And be sure of this, Cardinal. The Queen told me you are returning to Monte Cassino. Bon Voyage. And may the Lord keep you in his care. (*at the moment of the King's abrupt goodbye to Ruffo Vanni advances and bows very low.*)

VANNI: Sire—

KING: Ah, it's you, Marquis. I hope that your courts are not dozing.

VANNI: Yesterday, they executed four hundred rebels. But the arrival of Your Majesty is going to rekindle our zeal for the good cause. And if the King deigns to be present in person at the act of justice which is prepared to take place here in an hour— Your presence would have a prodigious effect on the faithful people.

KING: That's an idea.

VANNI: They are great offenders. We are going to strike Cyrillo, the Count Caraffa, and the Chevalier San Felice.

KING: San Felice. I will be there. Count on me, Mr. Marquis Vanni. (*he leaves*)

RUFFO: (*to his officers*) Gentlemen, we have nothing to do in Naples. (*they lead in the Cardinal's capering mule. As he is about to mount, Fra Pacifico comes in, a pilgrims staff in his hand, approaches and grabs the Cardinal's purple robe.*)

FRA PACIFICO: Milord.

RUFFO: (*turning*) Ah! Fra Pacifico. I am happy to see you. You've been a good servant of the King. What do you want from me?

FRA PACIFICO: My dismissal, Eminence and the road to Jerusalem.

RUFFO: You are going to the Holy Land? To do penitence? Have you committed some great sin?

FRA PACIFICO: I am afraid of having done so.

RUFFO: That's fine. I will commend you to the Captain of an English ship leaving for Saint John of Acre.

FRA PACIFICO: (*violently*) I want nothing from the English. They are heretics.

RUFFO: (*considering him attentively*) Have you only that to reproach them with?

FRA PACIFICO: (*fist extended toward the Port*) And then—they hanged my Admiral.

RUFFO: Caracciolo. And it's that crime you were going to demand pardon for them?

FRA PACIFICO: Not for them. For myself. Didn't I contribute to it by serving a bad cause?

RUFFO: What are you saying? The cause of the King?

FRA PACIFICO: What's it matter? The cause that put my Admiral to death—who was justice, honor, loyalty in person—cannot be a good cause.

RUFFO: Go then. Take this purse. You will pass Scutori. You will embark at Salonika. Go. Do your devotions at the Holy Sepulchre. And pray to God to pardon you your sin, and you will pray him to pardon mine at the same time.

FRA PACIFICO: (*astonished, stepping back*) Your Eminence also has committed a sin?

RUFFO: Alas, yes. I fear it. A great fault. God who reads in the depths of hearts may, perhaps, pardon me. But posterity never will.

FRA PACIFICO: (*stupefied*) And what?

RUFFO: I set back on his throne, from which Providence had toppled him, a perjured, cruel and stupid King. Go, brother, go, and pray for us both. (*The Cardinal mounts his mule and is followed by his escort of Calabrians. Fra Pacifico remains thoughtful for a moment, then leaves by the left. The square is empty.*)

BECCAIO: (*slipping from the prison*) No one. He's gone. I can get back to the Vieux Marche. (*But as he goes into a side street , the Penitent rises and seizes him.*) Mercy. I am dead.

MICHELE: (*pulling back his hood*) You said it. Look at this knife. It's yours. It is still red with the blood of Angiolina.

BECCAIO: (*trying to get loose*) Are you mad? For one woman more or less? Is that something for two friends to quarrel about?

MICHELE: Have you said your prayers?

BECCAIO: (*who has pulled his knife, tries to hit Michele*) Here, there's my Misere. (*Michele parries the blow, but he is forced to release Beccaio who runs towards the ramp. With a leap Michele catches him and plunges his knife in Beccaio's throat.*)

BECCAIO: (*falling on the terrace*) I am dead! A priest!

MICHELE: (*rolling him around the parapet*) Without confession, bandit. Without confession. (*Michele has rid himself of his penitent's robe and comes face to face downstage with Nanno, Luisa and Salvato who witnessed the end of the struggle.*)

LUISA: It's Michele.

MICHELE: Who's paid his debts before bidding life goodbye.

LUISA: What do you mean?

MICHELE: The fatherland is butchered, my heart is dead. I've decided to go before the rope which you so well predicted for me, Nanno. And to end in good company. I am going to find the Chevalier in that cage. At the least, he can find support in my arms to mount the scaffold.

LUISA: The Chevalier? Living? A prisoner?

MICHELE: You didn't know?

NANNO: What's it matter? Don't waste time in vain words. The hour is favorable. Come.

LUISA: No, Nanno. I won't leave any more. For me to abandon him to his executioners! My place is beside him. Pardon me, Salvato.

SALVATO: Pardon you! O generous heart that doesn't fail. I understand you, my Luisa. Yes, duty lies there. It's there that we must proceed. No more than you do I want happiness built on remorse and shame. (*they go towards the prison with Michele. Nanno remains pensive. She notices Fragola.*)

NANNO: Fragola! Come! There is still a way to save them. (*They leave. At this moment the prison doors open and the bailiffs push Michele, Luisa and Salvato away. The crowd invades the square. On the scaffold, an executioner, dressed in red. At the foot of the scaffold a table is placed where Vanni sits with his two assessors. A circle opens in the crowd in front of the table. The prisoners are placed in it watched by Pasquale di Simone and his bailiffs.*)

THE LAZZARONI: Death to the Jacobins! To the gibbet!

HECTOR: You hear them? There's the reward of our sacrifice.

CYRILLO: It's not for these fools. It's for all humanity that we are dying. The blood of martyrs is a terrible dissolver of thrones.

VANNI: (*to his colleagues*) Gentlemen, we have a great task to fulfill today. These are the heads of this impious revolution that we are going to judge. And to complete the honor, our illustrious monarch has promised to be present at these trials. Yes, the great King Ferdinand. (*The King appears on the ramp and takes his place.*)

VOICES: (*shouting*) Long Live Nosey!

VANNI: Sire, the tribunal renders you deep thanks for this signal mark of your favor. The court is open.

KING: (*to D'Ascoli*) He really presides well.

VANNI: I call the accused, Hector Caraffa.

HECTOR: Prince d'Andrea.

VANNI: You fermented rebellion, stirred up the bourgeoisie, organized the Revolution. You were one of the principal leaders of the Jacobins.

HECTOR: And one of the victors at Civita-Castellana.

VANNI: You admit having served against your country.

HECTOR: Against King Ferdinand—which is quite different.

KING: Insolent!

VANNI: To death!

CROWD: To death! To Death! (*Caraffa is made to mount the scaffold accompanied by the bailiffs.*)

VANNI: Dominique Cyrillo. Your age and occupation.

CYRILLO: I am sixty years old. Under the monarchy I was a doctor. Under the republic, a representative of the people.

VANNI: And before me what are you?

CYRILLO: Before you, coward, I am a hero.

VANNI: To death!

CROWD: Bravo! To the gibbet with the Jacobins!

VANNI: Come forward, Chevalier San Felice. Do you confess you betrayed the cause of the King?

SAN FELICE: I admit my pity for these victims and my scorn for the executioners.

VANNI: I would like to have joined you in this warrant with your worthy spouse. But after the defeat she pusillanimously abandoned you. Without doubt to follow some lover.

SAN FELICE: Miserable clown!

LUISA: (*who has parted the crowd along with Michele and Salvato*) You are mistaken, Mr. Procurator-Fiscal, for here I am!

CROWD: La San Felice.

KING: La San Felice. By Jove, how this will rejoice the Queen.

SAN FELICE: Ah, Luisa, what have you done?

LUISA: Dead, I could only weep for you. Living, I've come to share your fate.

SAN FELICE: My child.

VANNI: La San Felice. General Salvato Palmieri. You've got them, gentlemen, these great criminals. They were the soul of this satanic republic.

ALL: To death! To death!

MICHELE: Move one of your humps, Mr. Fiscal. You are preventing me from seeing this good Nosey.

VANNI: You! You will swing first.

SALVATO: (*to the king*) You are triumphing, Nosey. And these infatuated people are making themselves the accomplice of their tyrant. But take care. The day is near perhaps when it will understand its mistake and then will itself snatch the axe from the hands of your executioners, force you anew to take the road to exile to flee its anger and its justice.

KING: He threatens, I think. By Saint Janvier, I answer cursed Jacobins. I will make you all die, your women and your children. So that the seed will be lost. Who will come to trouble my repose after that?

SALVATO: Your remorse!

KING: (*laughing*) My remorse! Come on! My remorse!

SALVATO: You laugh, King Ferdinand. Yesterday you were laughing on board the *Thunderer* in the midst of the party you were giving in honor of Admiral Nelson when suddenly the laughter froze on your lips and you recoiled, trembling with horror and terror. It was because your crime was rising before you. Because surging from the waves of the sea, the cadaver of the Noble Caracciolo came to show his pale tortured face to his executioner.

KING: (*with terror*) Ah, the Admiral.

SALVATO: From this day, Ferdinand you will belong to the ghost of Caracciolo. Double your guards, make your bailiffs watch. They won't prevent the vengeful shades of your victims from rising, implacable at your bedstead, and from peopling your sleepless nights with sinister and threatening passage.

KING: Shut up! Shut up!

SALVATO: In vain will you attempt to flee this torment. It will follow you everywhere, wretch! Until the day when, maddened by rage, worn out by terror, exhausted by insomnia, you will abruptly die, choking on the generous blood of those you've butchered.

KING: (*moving away*) Ah! Let him be shut up. Deliver me, Vanni.

VANNI: Master Donato, do your duty. (*All the condemned are forced onto the scaffold. Master Donato, the executioner places a rope around the neck of Michele. The court and the King's suite move to the right to better enjoy the spectacle. At this moment a drumbeat can be heard. At first weak but swiftly approaching.*)

KING: (*cupping his ear*) What's that?

VANNI: I don't know, Sire. Some patrol.

ARIOLA: Why, they are beating the charge.

PASQUALE: (*on the top of the ramp*) Alert! Those are French drums.

KING: The French! What do you mean the French? (*cannon fire*)

PASQUALE: It's the fort of Saint Elmo opening up on us.

KING: The French! My horse! Save yourselves if you can!

(*He runs out to the right followed by D'Ascoli. The French begin to appear at the top of the ramparts. The crowd is forced back. Some rifle shots are fired. Nicolino appears at the head of the garrison of Saint Elmo forcing a passage through the crowd. The executioner and his helpers have fled leaving Michele with a rope around his neck and the other condemned on the scaffold.*)

PASQUALE: My word, Mr. Procurator-Fiscal. My men are showing their heels. It's fine time to make a retreat.

VANNI: To lose such a good catch! No! Ah, soldiers. Let the justice of the King be accomplished. Fire on the condemned.

(*A squad of royal soldiers obeys and fires on the condemned. San Felice throws himself in front of Luisa and he alone is hit. The French arrive clubbing and bayoneting the royal troops and emerge masters of the square.*)

NICOLINO: (*hugging Salvato*) You are saved. All the high town is ours. But we must hasten to reach Capua.

LUISA: (*sustaining San Felice*) Oh! My father!

SAN FELICE: You are free, I am dying happy.

MICHELE: (*who reappears with a rope around his neck and a saber in his hand. To Nanno*) I've been hanged. And here I am safe. Long live France!

SALVATO: Yes, Michele. Long live France! And long live the Republic!

(*Universal acclamations.*)

CURTAIN

ABOUT FRANK J. MORLOCK

FRANK J. MORLOCK has written and translated many plays since retiring from the legal profession in 1992. His translations have also appeared on Project Gutenberg, the Alexandre Dumas Père web page, Literature in the Age of Napoléon, Infinite Artistries.com, and Munsey's (formerly Blackmask). In 2006 he received an award from the North American Jules Verne Society for his translations of Verne's plays. He lives and works in Maryland and México.

www.ingramcontent.com/pod-product-compliance
Lightning Source LLC
LaVergne TN
LVHW091258080426
835510LV00007B/318